MASTERING
VISICALC

MASTERING VISICALC

Douglas Hergert

Berkeley • Paris • Düsseldorf

Cover art by Daniel Le Noury
Layout and design by Ingrid Owen

Apple is a registered trademark of Apple Computer, Inc.
DIF is a trademark of Software Arts, Inc.
IBM is a registered trademark of International Business Machines Corporation.
TRS-80 is a trademark of Tandy Corporation.
VisiCalc is a registered trademark of VisiCorp, Inc.

Library of Congress Card Number: 82-62005
ISBN 0-89588-090-3
Printed in the United States of America
10 9 8 7 6 5 4 3 2 1

To my parents

TABLE OF CONTENTS

ACKNOWLEDGEMENTS

Sincere thanks go to Salley Oberlin and Elaine Foster for their technical, editorial, and moral support during the preparation of this book. I also want to thank the following members of the Sybex production staff for their sensitive work: Valerie Brewster, Margaret Cusick, Michael Howard, Sharon Leong, Ingrid Owen, Donna Scanlon, Hilda van Genderen, and Cheryl Wilcox.

INTRODUCTION

The "electronic spreadsheet" programs have quickly become one of the leading software applications for use on personal computers. These programs give us the capability to process hundreds of numbers at once, to find patterns, draw conclusions, and explore alternatives suggested by any kind of numerical data. Their power applies itself as well to the small numerical chores of private life as to the larger record-keeping, decision-making jobs of professional life. And most appealing of all, using these programs requires scarcely more technical knowledge or mathematical skill than is needed to operate a pocket calculator.

The VisiCalc® program, written by Software Arts, Inc., is certainly one of the best and most popular of these spreadsheet programs. Available for most of the major microcomputers on the market today, the VisiCalc program demonstrates the two most important qualities of the electronic spreadsheet: it is easy to use, yet flexible and versatile enough to solve a wide range of technical or nontechnical tasks.

Even more importantly, the creators of the VisiCalc program have taken the initiative to design a spreadsheet program that can share data easily and reliably with the other software tools that reside in the same microcomputer environment. This kind of outward friendliness is rare in the world of commercial software; too many programs are designed, intentionally, to be unapproachable, uncooperative, and monolithic with respect to other, competing, programs.

Mastering VisiCalc, then, is written for several levels of use:

- If you are a newcomer to the VisiCalc program, this book will guide you through the first steps of learning how to use the program for your own individual needs. You will find out how to enter data, and how to take advantage of all the major VisiCalc features.

- If you have already started using the VisiCalc program, but still have questions about some of its more advanced features, this book will be useful to you. You will find insight into the subtleties of the more difficult functions—such as @LOOKUP, @NVP, and the logical functions—and you will learn techniques for optimal use of the VisiCalc program.

- Finally, if you are ready to expand outward and begin using the VisiCalc program with other programs of your own design, this book offers a complete introduction to the use of DIF™ files for communicating data between VisiCalc and BASIC. Mastering this feature can be a challenge; but in the end, you will profit from vastly increased control over the data processing tasks you perform on your computer.

Chapter 1—*The VisiCalc Program and Your Computer*—sets the scene of this book. It presents several examples of what VisiCalc can do, and offers you a quick overview of the features of the program.

Chapter 2—*An Introduction to the VisiCalc Program*—gives you a complete, hands-on guided tour through the major VisiCalc commands. It shows you how to enter data, write formulas, and apply those formulas to entire rows and columns of data.

Chapter 3—*VisiCalc Functions, Part I*—teaches you how to use the most common functions, such as @SUM and @AVERAGE, and gives you an opportunity to study the action of the more advanced mathematical functions.

Chapter 4—*VisiCalc Functions, Part II*—helps you to explore the use of @LOOKUP and the logical functions, which sometimes seem mysterious to the beginner. Since some versions of the VisiCalc program do not include the logical functions, this chapter suggests several alternative techniques that can be used to simulate these functions.

Chapter 5—*Planning VisiCalc Spreadsheets*—is an essential chapter for all readers. It shows you how to develop generalized spreadsheets that will be of long-term value rather than one-time use. It also clarifies some potentially confusing concepts involving the way VisiCalc performs spreadsheet calculations.

The last three chapters of this book introduce DIF files as a means of sharing data between the VisiCalc program and BASIC. If you have never programmed in BASIC, or if you are a relative beginner, you should read Appendix B—*A Brief Look at BASIC*—before beginning these chapters.

Chapter 6—*DIF Files, Part I*—describes and illustrates the structure of the Data Interface Format (DIF™). It also presents a BASIC program that will display any DIF file on the screen of your computer. This program, and the programs that follow in Chapters 7 and 8, require certain file-handling facilities that are expressed in different instructions by various versions of BASIC. Appendix A supplies these instructions for the BASICs of three popular personal computers—Apple® ,TRS-80™, and the IBM® Personal Computer.

Chapter 7—*DIF Files, Part II*—discusses situations that may call for the combined powers of VisiCalc and BASIC. This chapter shows you how a BASIC program can achieve access to the data from a VisiCalc spreadsheet.

Chapter 8—*DIF Files, Part III*—illustrates the final step in VisiCalc/BASIC data exchange. This chapter presents a tool that may prove valuable to you for many data processing situations—a BASIC program designed to *sort* VisiCalc spreadsheet data.

In sum, the goals of *Mastering VisiCalc* are twofold: first, to teach you how to use the VisiCalc program, and second, to help you explore the use of VisiCalc teamed with other programs on your personal computer.

CHAPTER ONE

THE VISICALC PROGRAM AND YOUR COMPUTER

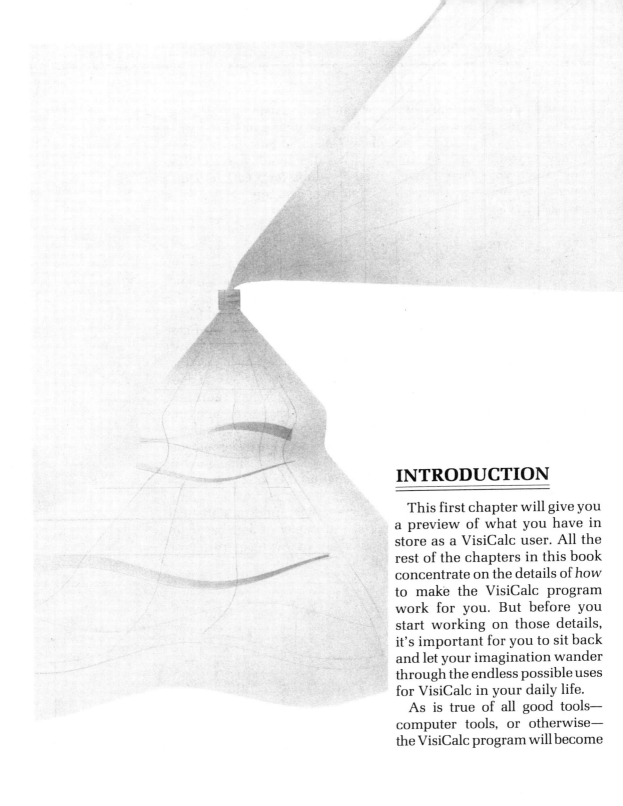

INTRODUCTION

This first chapter will give you a preview of what you have in store as a VisiCalc user. All the rest of the chapters in this book concentrate on the details of *how* to make the VisiCalc program work for you. But before you start working on those details, it's important for you to sit back and let your imagination wander through the endless possible uses for VisiCalc in your daily life.

As is true of all good tools—computer tools, or otherwise—the VisiCalc program will become more and more valuable to you as your skill in using it increases. This chapter will suggest some elementary uses of VisiCalc, as well as several more advanced applications. For the moment, imagine yourself as a seasoned VisiCalc user, ready to start thinking about your own individual applications for VisiCalc. Don't worry yet about the *how* of VisiCalc use; just concentrate for a while on the *what*.

WHAT VISICALC CAN DO FOR YOU

Think of any group of numbers you have used, compiled, or just come into contact with in your daily life at work or at home. The numbers might represent anything at all—from household financial information, to business accounting records, to scientific or statistical data. Typically, we see such numbers arranged in rows and columns as in Figure 1.1. Without descriptive labels or a title, the numbers are meaningless; however, their tabular format does tell us something: the rows and columns obviously represent categories of some kind, and the numbers clearly have some central theme or reason for being arranged together in table form.

Given a tabular set of numbers like this, there are three categories of tasks to perform to make the numbers useful and meaningful.

First, you may have to do some *calculating* based on the numbers in the table. The results of your calculations could include summarizing the data by finding totals or averages; finding statistical trends in the data; producing whole new tables of data based on the numbers in the original table; or even answering questions or drawing conclusions from the data.

11.18	6.35	8.13	3.56	2.54	0.76	1.52	2.03	1.78	3.81	7.62	9.40
7.62	7.11	5.59	3.30	0.25	0.00	0.00	0.00	0.51	0.76	5.08	5.59
11.18	7.62	6.35	4.06	1.02	0.25	0.00	0.00	0.51	2.54	5.84	10.16
1.52	1.78	3.05	4.83	6.86	4.83	4.57	3.30	2.79	2.79	2.03	1.02
4.83	5.33	7.62	9.91	9.91	11.18	9.40	7.37	7.37	7.11	6.35	5.08
11.43	11.68	13.97	10.67	10.67	11.94	17.02	13.46	14.22	5.84	9.91	12.95
6.60	5.59	7.87	8.89	8.89	8.38	3.89	7.87	7.11	6.60	7.11	6.10
5.59	5.08	5.33	9.30	15.49	22.86	17.53	17.24	22.10	20.83	6.86	4.06
6.60	6.35	8.38	7.37	9.55	8.89	10.41	12.09	7.87	6.86	7.37	7.62
6.86	7.37	9.40	8.38	8.89	7.62	9.40	10.16	8.38	7.37	9.65	8.89

Figure 1.1: A Group of Numbers Arranged in Rows and Columns

Second, you will probably want to *present* the numbers so that their meaning and organization are immediately clear to anyone who looks at your table. You can do this by supplying labels for the rows and columns, writing a title at the top of the table, and perhaps also including a few words indicating the units or the scale of the numbers. You might need to round the numbers out to fewer decimal places, depending on what the numbers actually represent. Finally, you may even want to devise some visual representation of the numbers—a bar graph, for example—to make the presentation even clearer and more dramatic. The audience you could have in mind for this presentation might be your business associates, your colleagues on a project, your teachers or classmates, your family or friends.

The third basic task is *storing* the numbers. You must be able to keep this numerical information filed accurately and reliably, so that you can find it quickly whenever you need it. Or, in a more complicated situation, you may want to store different parts of the table in different places, rather than the whole table all in one place. Each part of the table might be destined for a different use, and so it would be very convenient to be able to store the data according to your eventual needs for it.

The VisiCalc program is a tool designed to help you perform these three tasks with exquisite simplicity, yet perfect reliability. Jobs that would take days to do by hand, or many hours with a pocket calculator, can be completed in minutes using VisiCalc. You don't have to be a computer programmer to understand how the VisiCalc program works. In fact, you can begin working with VisiCalc almost as soon as you have the program running on your computer—even before you understand everything that VisiCalc offers you. On the other hand, the more you learn about VisiCalc, the more effectively you can use it in coordination with the other tools available to you on your personal computer.

When you first start the VisiCalc program running on your computer you will see a vast array of empty rows and columns with hundreds of positions into which you can enter numbers, words (called "labels"), or even arithmetic formulas. The features of VisiCalc are designed to give you maximum control over the information that you type into the rows and columns. Since you can't see *all* of the rows and columns at one time, the screen of your computer becomes a "window" that you can move up and down the columns, or back and forth over rows. By moving the window through the information you have recorded, you can view exactly the information that you want at any given time.

For some examples of how the VisiCalc program can be used for the three basic tasks we have outlined—calculation, presentation, and storage—let's look at what we can do with the numbers we saw in Figure 1.1. A table of numbers only really has meaning when we give it labels and a title. So, let's develop three imaginary—but plausible—situations in which numbers like these might be used. In other words, we'll supply three different meanings to the same set of numbers. Although this may require a certain suspension of disbelief, it will illustrate an important point: the *meaning* of the numbers is irrelevant to the VisiCalc program, which, after all, only performs the commands and operations that you, the user, request.

The tables in Figures 1.2, 1.3, 1.4, and 1.5 were all created using the VisiCalc program. VisiCalc users tend to call such tables *spreadsheets*, or *worksheets*, but you can really call them anything you want. As you look at these tables, you'll notice the variety of changes that have been made on the original ten rows and twelve columns of numbers. Yet none of these spreadsheets took more than a few minutes to prepare. In the chapters ahead, you'll learn to create VisiCalc spreadsheets like these to meet your own needs. By the time you finish reading this book, you'll know exactly how to give instructions to the VisiCalc program to make it perform all the jobs illustrated in this chapter. But remember, for the moment don't worry about how to make the VisiCalc program work; just think about what you'll eventually want to use the VisiCalc program for.

VISICALC AT HOME

First consider a simple household application. Let's say you've been perplexed about where all your grocery money has been going, so you decide to keep track of your expenses over a period of twelve weeks. To do this, you have divided your expenses into ten different categories (miscellaneous, cereals, milk and eggs, sundries, cat food, and so on), and each week you have recorded the amounts you spent in each category. It is now the end of the twelve week period, and you want a summary of your expenditures. Specifically, you would like to know:

- the total amount you spent each week, and the total amount you spent for each category over the whole period of twelve weeks;
- the percent of the total period expenditures represented by each category;
- the average amount you spent per week for each category.

You start up the VisiCalc program on your computer, and you type in the numbers you've been recording over the twelve weeks. You include a title and labels for the categories and the weeks on the spreadsheet you are creating. Then, by typing in a few simple formulas in the format that VisiCalc understands, you quickly have all the information you require. Figure 1.2 shows how it might look.

```
                      WEEKLY GROCERY EXPENSES
                       30 MAY TO 21 AUGUST
==============================================================
         WEEK #1 WEEK #2 WEEK #3 WEEK #4 WEEK #5 WEEK #6 WEEK #7 WEEK #8
         ======= ======= ======= ======= ======= ======= ======= =======
MISC       11.18    6.35    8.13    3.56    2.54    0.76    1.52    2.03
CEREALS     7.62    7.11    5.59    3.30    0.25    0.00    0.00    0.00
MLK/EGGS   11.18    7.62    6.35    4.06    1.02    0.25    0.00    0.00
CAT FOOD    1.52    1.78    3.05    4.83    6.86    4.83    4.57    3.30
SUNDRIES    4.83    5.33    7.62    9.91    9.91   11.18    9.40    7.37
PRODUCE    11.43   11.68   13.97   10.67   10.67   11.94   17.02   13.46
CIGARETS    6.60    5.59    7.87    8.89    8.89    8.38    3.89    7.87
MEAT        5.59    5.08    5.33    9.30   15.49   22.86   17.53   17.24
PASTRIES    6.60    6.35    8.38    7.37    9.55    8.89   10.41   12.09
LIQUOR      6.86    7.37    9.40    8.38    8.89    7.62    9.40   10.16
**TOTALS   73.41   64.26   75.69   70.27   74.07   76.71   73.74   73.52


==============================================================
         WEEK #9 WEEK#10 WEEK#11 WEEK#12  TOTALS     %     AVE.
         ======= ======= ======= =======  ======     =     ====
MISC        1.78    3.81    7.62    9.40    58.68     7     4.89
CEREALS     0.51    0.76    5.08    5.59    35.81     4     2.98
MLK/EGGS    0.51    2.54    5.84   10.16    49.53     6     4.13
CAT FOOD    2.79    2.79    2.03    1.02    39.37     5     3.28
SUNDRIES    7.37    7.11    6.35    5.08    91.46    11     7.62
PRODUCE    14.22    5.84    9.91   12.95   143.76    17    11.98
CIGARETS    7.11    6.60    7.11    6.10    84.90    10     7.08
MEAT       22.10   20.83    6.86    4.06   152.27    18    12.69
PASTRIES    7.87    6.86    7.37    7.62    99.36    12     8.28
LIQUOR      8.38    7.37    9.65    8.89   102.37    12     8.53
**TOTALS   72.64   64.51   67.82   70.87   857.51   100    71.46
```

Figure 1.2: A Household Application of the Numbers

Of course, what you decide to *do* with all this information is up to you. VisiCalc can't make the decisions for you to cut expenses. The job of the VisiCalc program, rather, is to present you with the facts and figures quickly and simply so *you* can concentrate on decision making.

VISICALC AT THE OFFICE

The next application is in a business context. Let's say you are the sales manager for a small company, and you have been studying the performance of each of your ten salespeople over the past twelve months. Now that the year is over, you want to see who your most valuable people have been. You also want to calculate total salaries and commissions for the year; and, incidentally, it is time to award bonuses.

As you start up the VisiCalc program and begin entering the monthly sales figures for each person, you realize that you might end up having to let go of a couple of the weakest performers in the group. You'll have to justify your decision to your own boss, and you know that the most dramatic way to present the total picture will be with a bar graph of total annual sales for each salesperson.

Figure 1.3 shows the beginning of the spreadsheet that you start preparing. The names of your salespeople appear on the left, the months from January to December appear along the top, and the title explains the purpose of the table. Notice that the sales figures are in units of a thousand dollars. (This convention simplifies data entry, without seriously reducing accuracy.)

You next instruct VisiCalc to compute the total monthly sales (by summing up the columns) and the total sales for each person (by summing up the rows). Then, with a few quick keystrokes, you create a bar graph based on the latter totals.

Next, you need to calculate salaries. Your salespeople work on a $1000 monthly base salary, plus a 5% commission on sales. You use this formula to create a "salary plus commission" column on your spreadsheet.

Finally, there are the bonuses to determine. You award year-end bonuses to each salesperson according to total sales for the year. Your bonus schedule looks like this:

annual sales	*bonus*
$ 0 to $ 49,999	$ 250
$ 50,000 to $ 74,999	$1,000
$ 75,000 to $ 99,999	$1,500
$100,000 to $124,999	$2,250
$125,000 to $149,999	$3,000
$150,000 or greater	$3,500

To make this schedule available to your VisiCalc spreadsheet in the simplest way possible, you enter what is called a "look-up table." (We'll study the LOOKUP function in Chapter 4.) Referring to this table, VisiCalc can easily create a bonus column, and then a total salary column for your salespeople.

```
                    MONTHLY SALES BY SALESPERSON
                       (THOUSANDS OF DOLLARS)
==================================================================
             JAN    FEB    MAR    APR    MAY    JUN    JUL    AUG
             ===    ===    ===    ===    ===    ===    ===    ===
BAKER      11.18   6.35   8.13   3.56   2.54   0.76   1.52   2.03
SMITH       7.62   7.11   5.59   3.30   0.25   0.00   0.00   0.00
FLINT      11.18   7.62   6.35   4.06   1.02   0.25   0.00   0.00
BROWN       1.52   1.78   3.05   4.83   6.86   4.83   4.57   3.30
VERN        4.83   5.33   7.62   9.91   9.91  11.18   9.40   7.37
MARLOW     11.43  11.68  13.97  10.67  10.67  11.94  17.02  13.46
HARPER      6.60   5.59   7.87   8.89   8.89   8.38   3.89   7.87
FLEMING     5.59   5.08   5.33   9.30  15.49  22.86  17.53  17.24
NASH        6.60   6.35   8.38   7.37   9.55   8.89  10.41  12.09
WHITE       6.86   7.37   9.40   8.38   8.89   7.62   9.40  10.16


=========================================
             SEP    OCT    NOV    DEC
             ===    ===    ===    ===
BAKER       1.78   3.81   7.62   9.40
SMITH       0.51   0.76   5.08   5.59
FLINT       0.51   2.54   5.84  10.16
BROWN       2.79   2.79   2.03   1.02
VERN        7.37   7.11   6.35   5.08
MARLOW     14.22   5.84   9.91  12.95
HARPER      7.11   6.60   7.11   6.10
FLEMING    22.10  20.83   6.86   4.06
NASH        7.87   6.86   7.37   7.62
WHITE       8.38   7.37   9.65   8.89
```

Figure 1.3: A Business Application

Your complete spreadsheet is shown in Figure 1.4. Studying
the total salaries and the bar graph, you see immediately who is
doing well and who is not.

```
                    MONTHLY SALES BY SALESPERSON
                      (THOUSANDS OF DOLLARS)
================================================================
            JAN    FEB    MAR    APR    MAY    JUN    JUL    AUG
            ===    ===    ===    ===    ===    ===    ===    ===
BAKER      11.18   6.35   8.13   3.56   2.54   0.76   1.52   2.03
SMITH       7.62   7.11   5.59   3.30   0.25   0.00   0.00   0.00
FLINT      11.18   7.62   6.35   4.06   1.02   0.25   0.00   0.00
BROWN       1.52   1.78   3.05   4.83   6.86   4.83   4.57   3.30
VERN        4.83   5.33   7.62   9.91   9.91  11.18   9.40   7.37
MARLOW     11.43  11.68  13.97  10.67  10.67  11.94  17.02  13.46
HARPER      6.60   5.59   7.87   8.89   8.89   8.38   3.89   7.87
FLEMING     5.59   5.08   5.33   9.30  15.49  22.86  17.53  17.24
NASH        6.60   6.35   8.38   7.37   9.55   8.89  10.41  12.09
WHITE       6.86   7.37   9.40   8.38   8.89   7.62   9.40  10.16
**TOTALS   73.41  64.26  75.69  70.27  74.07  76.71  73.74  73.52


================================================================
            SEP    OCT    NOV    DEC   TOTALS SAL+COM BONUS TOT SAL
            ===    ===    ===    ===   ====== ======= ===== =======
BAKER       1.78   3.81   7.62   9.40   58.68  14.93   1.00  15.93
SMITH       0.51   0.76   5.08   5.59   35.81  13.79   0.25  14.04
FLINT       0.51   2.54   5.84  10.16   49.53  14.48   0.25  14.73
BROWN       2.79   2.79   2.03   1.02   39.37  13.97   0.25  14.22
VERN        7.37   7.11   6.35   5.08   91.46  16.57   1.50  18.07
MARLOW     14.22   5.84   9.91  12.95  143.76  19.19   3.00  22.19
HARPER      7.11   6.60   7.11   6.10   84.90  16.25   1.50  17.75
FLEMING    22.10  20.83   6.86   4.06  152.27  19.61   3.50  23.11
NASH        7.87   6.86   7.37   7.62   99.36  16.97   1.50  18.47
WHITE       8.38   7.37   9.65   8.89  102.37  17.12   2.25  19.37
**TOTALS   72.64  64.51  67.82  70.87  857.51


BAKER    ******                      BONUS TABLE
SMITH    ****                        ===========
FLINT    *****                          0.00    0.25
BROWN    ****                           50.00    1.00
VERN     ********                       75.00    1.50
MARLOW   **************                100.00    2.25
HARPER   *******                       125.00    3.00
FLEMING  ***************              150.00    3.50
NASH     *********
WHITE    *********
```

Figure 1.4: The Complete Business Application

THE SCIENTIFIC VISICALC

In the third spreadsheet example we turn toward the scientific realm. Let's say you are working on a research project that requires rainfall statistics for several dozen large U.S. cities. You have begun gathering data for some of the cities, and you have organized the information in a VisiCalc table that you have called "Monthly Normal Precipitation (in centimeters)." This table appears in Figure 1.5. (Recognize the numbers? The table actually contains the same figures as the tables in the previous two examples, but they look different because they have been rounded off to the nearest integer. This rounding operation was performed instantly by a single VisiCalc global format command. We'll study this command in Chapter 2.)

Your assignment in this project is to continue gathering data

```
                  MONTHLY NORMAL PRECIPITATION
                        (IN CENTIMETERS)
         ===================================================
            JAN    FEB    MAR    APR    MAY    JUN    JUL    AUG
            ===    ===    ===    ===    ===    ===    ===    ===
HONOLULU     11     6      8      4      3      1      2      2
LOS ANGL      8     7      6      3      0      0      0      0
SAN FRAN     11     8      6      4      1      0      0      0
DENVER        2     2      3      5      7      5      5      3
ST.LOUIS      5     5      8     10     10     11      9      7
NEW ORLN     11    12     14     11     11     12     17     13
CLEVELND      7     6      8      9      9      8      4      8
MIAMI         6     5      5      9     15     23     18     17
WASH DC       7     6      8      7     10      9     10     12
NEW YORK      7     7      9      8      9      8      9     10



         =================================================
            SEP    OCT    NOV    DEC   TOTALS
            ===    ===    ===    ===   ======
HONOLULU     2      4      8      9      59
LOS ANGL     1      1      5      6      36
SAN FRAN     1      3      6     10      50
DENVER       3      3      2      1      39
ST.LOUIS     7      7      6      5      91
NEW ORLN    14      6     10     13     144
CLEVELND     7      7      7      6      85
MIAMI       22     21      7      4     152
WASH DC      8      7      7      8      99
NEW YORK     8      7     10      9     102
```

Figure 1.5: A Scientific Application

for additional cities until all the specified cities have been covered. When the data is complete, you have several tasks to perform. You have to compute some statistical values from the data (means, variances, standard deviations, and so on). Then you are to *sort* the table in two different ways. Sorting means arranging data in some specified order. You must present the data sorted first in alphabetical order by the names of the cities, then in descending order of the total annual precipitation of each city. In other words, you are to present the data twice, each presentation destined for a different use.

Let's say you have taken the time to get to know your computer fairly well. As a result, you know that the VisiCalc program is only one of the powerful problem-solving tools that your computer offers you. Another one of these tools, a programming language called BASIC, is also easy to use, and, as it turns out, can be teamed up with the VisiCalc program to complete certain tasks faster and more efficiently than would be possible using either tool alone.

Upon reflection, you decide that the tasks before you—calculating statistical values, sorting the data, and presenting the rainfall tables in a neat, orderly way—will be most convenient to perform if you do in fact use the combined powers of the VisiCalc program and BASIC. The VisiCalc program is ideally suited for the *input and output* tasks—that is to say, entering all the data into your computer, and preparing the final presentation of the data. However, some of the statistical computations, and certainly the sorting operations, could prove to be a bit clumsy in VisiCalc. In any event, you know that many simple BASIC programs are available that will take care of these tasks easily and gracefully.

The only problem is this: how do you transfer the rainfall data between VisiCalc and BASIC? Is it possible to make data available to more than one of the tools on your computer?

Once again, the VisiCalc program comes through with a solution to the problem. VisiCalc provides a method for storing data from a spreadsheet onto a special kind of disk file, called a DIF file. DIF stands for Data Interchange Format. The reason DIF is so special is that it stores data in such a way that it can be read by the VisiCalc program *or* by a BASIC program that you write yourself (or, for that matter, by any number of other programs that you may use on your computer.) In short, DIF files provide a means of trading data between various programming tools that you may find yourself using. We will explore the significance and the use of DIF files in the last three chapters of this book.

Briefly, here is a summary of the steps that you'll follow to complete all the required tasks associated with your rainfall table:

- First, you'll use the VisiCalc program to create a table like the one you see in Figure 5.5. When you are ready to perform the intermediate tasks—calculating statistics, and sorting the data—you'll instruct VisiCalc to create a DIF file containing the rainfall data.
- Next, you'll use BASIC programs designed to read the DIF file and to perform the calculating and sorting tasks. Chapters 7 and 8 will provide you with two complete BASIC programs designed for these purposes, and all the information you will need in order to use the programs. (In addition, Appendix B offers a brief introduction to BASIC, in case you are new to BASIC programming.)
- Then you will use one of these two BASIC programs (the one presented in Chapter 8) to create a new DIF file of *sorted* rainfall data. So, the final step for you will be to instruct the VisiCalc program to read this new DIF file onto a spreadsheet, giving you exactly the kind of data presentation that you require.

The essential point is this: the VisiCalc program allows you to *share* spreadsheet data with other programming tools available on your microcomputer. As a result, you can take advantage of the features of more than one of these programming tools to solve complicated programs.

A QUICK LOOK AT THINGS TO COME

We have now examined three different situations in which the VisiCalc program would help you to calculate, present, and store large tables of numbers. The key to making all these things happen is a set of simple commands that you type on your keyboard. These commands tell the VisiCalc program exactly what you want it to do with the numbers you have entered onto the spreadsheet. Like everything else about VisiCalc, the method of giving commands is first of all characterized by its simplicity. VisiCalc gives you a *command line*, which displays the options you have for manipulating your VisiCalc spreadsheet. When you are using the VisiCalc program, you can look at this command line by pressing the slash (/) key on your computer's keyboard. You will see the following line at the top of your screen:

COMMAND: BCDEFGIMPRSTVW —

Each one of the characters on the command line (the letters, plus the character " — ") represents one of the VisiCalc features. To use one of these features, you simply press the appropriate character key on your keyboard while the command line is in view on the screen.

To learn to use the VisiCalc program, then, you basically have to learn what each of these commands does. That is the task ahead of you as you read this book. Figure 1.6 gives a brief summary of the functions of the commands. You may want to glance at this summary now, so you'll have a general feeling for the kinds of functions they perform, but, don't worry about trying to memorize the commands at this point. Later, when you've had a bit of experience with using the VisiCalc program, you can use Figure 1.6 as a reference table to remind you what each of the commands does.

To summarize the VisiCalc commands, we might divide them into three main functional groups—calculation, control, and storage. The main calculation feature is the replication command, /R. The control commands allow you to *delete* information from the spreadsheet (/B, /C, /D), to *revise* or *reformat* information (/E, /F, /G, /I, /M), and to *control* the portion of the spreadsheet that you see on the screen (/W, /T). Finally, the storage commands include both disk storage (/S) and output to a printer (/P).

/B   B stands for *blank*. This command lets you erase any single position on the VisiCalc screen—whether that position contains a label or a numerical value.

/C   This command erases (or *clears*) the entire VisiCalc screen, so that you can start fresh on a new spreadsheet.

Figure 1.6: A Brief Summary of the VisiCalc Commands (continues)

/D This command allows you to *delete* an entire row or column of your spreadsheet.

/E With this command you can *edit* the contents of any position on the VisiCalc screen. (Note that some versions of VisiCalc do not have this feature.)

/F The *format* command lets you specify how you want data to be presented on your VisiCalc spreadsheet. We have seen that numerical data can be presented in decimal or integer form. Information can also be right- or left-justified within a position. The format command is also used to create bar graphs.

/G G stands for *global*. This command allows you to format the entire VisiCalc screen, rather than just a single position on the screen. You can also use the global command to increase the number of character-spaces available in each column of the screen. (In addition, /G provides some features that concern numerical calculations.)

/I I lets you *insert* a row or column anywhere on the screen.

/M With this command you can *move* any row or column to a new position on your spreadsheet.

/P This command allows you to *print* your spreadsheet on paper.

/R This is perhaps the single most important feature that VisiCalc offers you. It is also probably the command that you'll use the most. R stands for *replicate*; when you have typed an arithmetic formula into VisiCalc, this command lets you *apply* that formula to whole rows and columns of data, instantly. This command is the essence of the VisiCalc program.

/S The *storage* command lets you save both VisiCalc and DIF files on disk, and load them from disk back into VisiCalc.

Figure 1.6: A Brief Summary of the VisiCalc Commands (continues)

/T   With this command you can establish rows or columns of information that will remain stationary on the screen, even when you adjust the window position on the spreadsheet. Typically these rows or columns are labels, or *titles* that you don't wish to lose from sight as you move around the spreadsheet.

/V   Tells you what *version* of VisiCalc you are working on.

/W   Allows you to split the screen into two *windows* so that you can view two different parts of your spreadsheet at a time.

/—   You will use this command when you want to draw lines across the worksheet to improve clarity. Each of the tables in Figures 1.2 to 1.5 has a double line separating the title from the rest of the table. These lines were drawn by the /— command.

Figure 1.6: A Brief Summary of the VisiCalc Commands

VERSIONS OF THE VISICALC PROGRAM

The VisiCalc program has been designed to work on many different microcomputers; however, on each different computer some details of the program may vary. These variations often have more to do with the computers themselves than with the VisiCalc program. For example, the appearance of the "window" on the worksheet, which you see on your screen, varies. The number of columns and rows that you can fit onto your screen at any one time, and the shape of the *cursor* are not the same for each computer. The cursor, as we will see in Chapter 2, is a position indicator that tells you your location on the spreadsheet. You can move the cursor in four directions—up, down, left, right—but the keys that you use to move it are different for each computer. Some computers have four different direction keys for moving the cursor; others have only two direction keys, which must be toggled into vertical or horizontal modes.

All in all, none of these variations make the versions of the VisiCalc program *essentially* different from one another. But you will have to get used to handling these different details when you start using your version of VisiCalc on your own computer.

There are, however, a few more important variations, involving features that may be missing from some versions of VisiCalc. For example, some versions do not have the edit (/E) command. Some versions are also missing several of the VisiCalc *functions* that we will discuss in Chapter 4. When we examine these particular features, we will try to explore alternate methods of accomplishing these tasks.

The most serious variation is that a few versions of the VisiCalc program do not support the DIF file storage feature. If you have one of these versions, you will not be able to create DIF files to share data with other programs. Fortunately, most versions of VisiCalc do support DIF.

MEMORY

The way in which your computer stores a spreadsheet in its internal memory generally need not concern you, as a VisiCalc user. The one time you must worry about memory space is when you start running out of it. The VisiCalc screen gives you an indicator of how much memory space you have left during the creation of any spreadsheet. This indicator is an integer that appears in the upper-right hand corner of your screen. It represents the number of remaining *kilobytes* of memory storage space. (A *byte* is the amount of memory space required to store one character; a kilobyte is 1024 bytes.) When you first begin running the VisiCalc program, this number may be large or small depending on how much memory your computer has. As you begin creating a spreadsheet, the number gets smaller and smaller, indicating that you are taking up some of the available memory. If your computer only has a small amount of memory, then of course you will be limited to small worksheets, with relatively little data. In Chapter 6 we will discuss a technique that can be used for partially overcoming the limitations of small internal memory. This method involves storing sections of worksheets in DIF files and then combining these sections on new worksheets.

When you run out of memory, VisiCalc replaces the memory-indicator with the letters "OM".

VISICALC AND BASIC

What we have seen so far is that VisiCalc relieves you of the tedium of many repetitive number-processing tasks and helps you create tables and graphs much more quickly than you could possibly prepare them by hand. And the great charm of using the VisiCalc program is its simplicity. Perhaps one of the main reasons that so many personal computer users are attracted to VisiCalc is that it doesn't require knowledge of a programming language.

Does this mean, then, that a tool like the VisiCalc program can replace microcomputer programming languages—such as BASIC and Pascal—altogether? Obviously not, but a valid question remains: Given the variety of tools available in the software repertoire of your computer, how do you decide when to use one tool rather than another?

One way to answer this question is to recall what kind of computer you're using—a *personal* computer. This means that the way you use your computer to solve problems is not defined by the manufacturers or even by the software writers, but rather by *you*. The computer is controlled by your intelligence, your creativity and ingenuity, and your personal preferences about the best way to handle any given task. (In addition, the computer usually responds quite avidly to your mistakes.)

Since you are in control, it is clearly to your advantage to have as many resources at your disposal as possible. True, you can do many exciting things with the VisiCalc program alone, but you can do even more with VisiCalc *plus* BASIC. This will be one of the continuing themes of this book; learning VisiCalc is fun and rewarding, but even more important is learning how to fit Visi-Calc into the whole context of your personal computer use.

If you don't know anything about BASIC yet, don't worry. Conquer one castle at a time; before you know it the whole kingdom will be yours.

You can read, understand, and use just about everything in this book without a background in BASIC programming. In the last three chapters of the book we will present some BASIC programs that read and create DIF files, and thus communicate indirectly with VisiCalc. You can use such programs without understanding fully how they work; or, you can take the time to study them, revise them, and adapt them to your own needs. Meanwhile,

Appendix B provides a brief summary of BASIC, along with a few notes about the differences between accomplishing a task in BASIC and completing the same job with VisiCalc. As you read this description of BASIC programming it will be natural for you to start comparing BASIC with the VisiCalc program. VisiCalc conveniently makes many of the details of programming completely invisible to you. Using VisiCalc, you don't have to think about how data storage relates to the logic of the program. Repetitive computation is as easy as typing "/R". And, perhaps most clearly to the point, *input and output are really simultaneous operations in VisiCalc.* You don't have to input a group of data and then think carefully about how you're going to display them; rather, you are actually creating your output table as you input the data.

On the other hand, the more you use the VisiCalc program, the more likely you are to run into situations where VisiCalc doesn't quite answer your needs, or where using VisiCalc seems to make the task harder, rather than easier. This does not in any way decrease the value of VisiCalc. A carpenter doesn't throw away his saw just because he discovers that it isn't very useful for hammering nails into wood. Any job is easier to perform once we learn to choose our tools appropriately. As you proceed forward in this book, and you begin to become comfortable with the mechanics of using the VisiCalc program, you should always keep an important question in the back of your mind: What kinds of applications are ideally suited to the features of VisiCalc, and which ones would be better suited to another microcomputer tool or to a combination of tools?

THE OPERATING SYSTEM

The basic functions of your computer are controlled by a central software network, called the *operating system.* This system handles input and output; performs the housekeeping chores of maintaining files on disk; loads programs into the computer's memory and gets them to run; and controls the software that translates programming languages (like BASIC and Pascal) into machine code that the computer can execute.

When you insert the VisiCalc diskette in your disk drive and turn on your computer, one of two things might happen, depending on your version of the program. Either your operating system will load the VisiCalc program and run it, so that you will see the VisiCalc window right away, or the operating system will give you a message indicating that it is waiting for your command. In the latter case, you will have to type the command that tells the operating system to load VisiCalc and run it. Often this command will simply be the name of the file that contains the VisiCalc program.

The VisiCalc /S command contains an option for quitting the VisiCalc program. It leaves you at the command level of your operating system. You may want to leave VisiCalc in this way for any number of reasons: to perform some disk operations that can't be done from within VisiCalc; to use an editor; to write or run a program in BASIC, or some other programming language. It is important to remember that if you leave VisiCalc, you lose the current worksheet that you have been working on. For this reason, you should always save your worksheet on disk before you exit from the VisiCalc program. This also is done with the /S command; we'll study the details of the command in Chapter 2.

OTHER SPREADSHEET PROGRAMS

Since the advent of the VisiCalc program, many competing spreadsheet programs have appeared on the market. Some of them are designed to be sold with specific computers, or to run on specific operating systems. For example, several run on CP/M, which is one of the most popular operating systems for microcomputers. As in other areas of microcomputer software, the great variety of commercial spreadsheet programs now available may tend to confuse the potential buyer. There's just too much to choose from, and making a careful and informed decision can be difficult.

There are, however, several important general questions you can ask about the capabilities of a spreadsheet program before you buy one for your computer. How easy is the program to learn to use? Does it seem to provide all the functions that you'll need for your particular use of the program? Does it have graphics capabilities? Does it communicate with other programs? In particular, does it create files that you can read conveniently from a

BASIC program? If you have a word processing program for your computer, can you easily incorporate spreadsheets into a word-processed text? If you have not yet bought a spreadsheet program, you will undoubtedly think of other questions to ask as you read this book.

SUMMARY

The VisiCalc program is a tool that you can use to banish permanently from your life the tedium of performing arithmetic on large sets of numbers. The program is oriented around rows and columns into which you can enter numbers, labels, or formulas. Input and output are actually a single operation in VisiCalc; you create a spreadsheet table by placing data exactly where you want it. If you specify calculations, VisiCalc can perform them for you instantly.

You control VisiCalc via a dozen single-letter commands that are displayed for you when you type the slash key. This represents the program's powerful simplicity, which has led to its tremendous popularity.

The VisiCalc program has been wisely designed to work along with other microcomputer tools; thus the ability to create DIF files is one of the essential characteristics of the program.

In Chapter 2 we will plunge into the details of VisiCalc's operation. If you own the VisiCalc program, now is the time to turn it on and follow along.

CHAPTER TWO

AN INTRODUCTION TO THE VISICALC PROGRAM

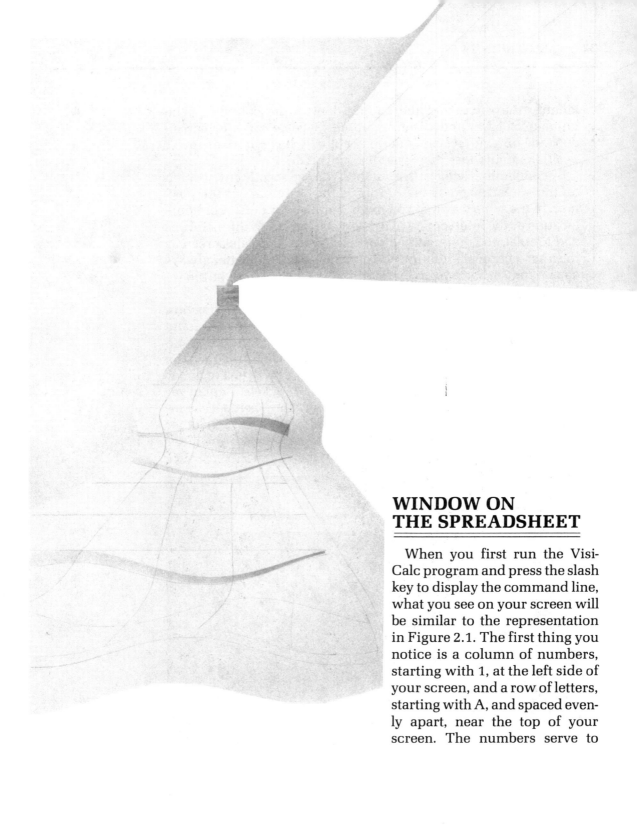

WINDOW ON
THE SPREADSHEET

When you first run the Visi-Calc program and press the slash key to display the command line, what you see on your screen will be similar to the representation in Figure 2.1. The first thing you notice is a column of numbers, starting with 1, at the left side of your screen, and a row of letters, starting with A, and spaced evenly apart, near the top of your screen. The numbers serve to identify the rows, and the letters identify the columns. (The number of rows and columns initially visible on your screen depends on your system; you may actually have more or fewer positions than those displayed in Figure 2.1.)

By combining a letter with a number, you can specify any position on the spreadsheet. Think of this as the "address" of the position. In the same way that you might identify your office or home location as the intersection of two streets (Main and Fifth, Spruce and Maple), so you identify a position on the VisiCalc screen as the intersection of a column and a row. The column letter always comes first in the address. For example, the position at the intersection of column C and row 9 is called C9.

When you first begin running the VisiCalc program, position A1, the upper-left position on the spreadsheet, contains a graphic display that is distinctive from the rest of the positions visible on the screen. Depending on your version of VisiCalc, either the whole position A1 will be highlighted with a light rectangle, or the position will be surrounded by two large brackets. Whichever graphic representation it is, you are looking at the VisiCalc *cursor*. This cursor tells you your current position on the screen. In other words, if you enter data onto the spreadsheet, the data you enter will be stored at the position marked by the cursor.

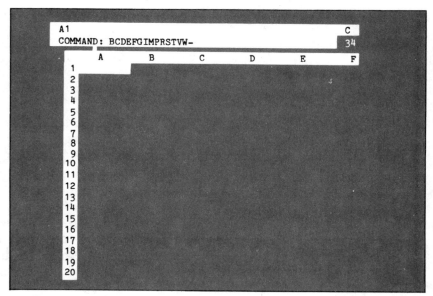

Figure 2.1: The VisiCalc Screen

Above the spreadsheet itself, at the top of your screen, are three lines of information that never disappear (although they may sometimes be empty), no matter where you move the cursor. These three lines give essential information about your spreadsheet, so it is important to learn how to read them correctly.

The first line, which we will call the contents line, displays the address and contents of the current position. At the beginning of your session with VisiCalc, before you have entered any data, this line simply indicates the current address of the cursor:

A1

Remember that the initial position of the cursor is A1, and the entire screen starts out blank. So what the contents line is telling you is that VisiCalc is ready to accept data, should you wish to enter it, at the empty position A1.

The second information line, called the prompt line, tells you what your current activity is, or what options you have at any given turn in the program. Since you have pressed the slash key, the command line is currently displayed as the prompt:

COMMAND: BCDEFGIMPRSTVW —

Many of these commands, as we will be seeing shortly, have subordinate command lines. Choosing one option leads to a subset of new options. The place to look for a display of these options is always the prompt line.

In addition, when you are entering data, the prompt line tells you what *type* of data you are entering. As soon as you type the first character of input, the prompt line will display:

VALUE

if you are entering numeric data, or:

LABEL

if you are entering nonnumeric data. Off hand, this may seem like an odd thing to have to be told; after all, you should know whether you are entering a number or a word. But this feature actually serves two purposes. First, it helps you understand the source of input errors. For example, if you begin typing a number and then inadvertently enter a nonnumeric character as part of the number, the VisiCalc program needs some way of alerting you to the discrepancy. Some systems will sound a bell in this situation.

When the bell goes off, you automatically look at the screen to see what you have done wrong. The word VALUE on the prompt line reminds you that you are in the process of entering a number, and hints that you have accidently typed a letter or some other non-numeric character.

The LABEL or VALUE message on the prompt line also serves a second purpose in some special situations. Sometimes you will want to enter a digit from 0 to 9, which you want to treat as a label rather than a number. Conversely, sometimes you will enter a letter that actually represents a value. The VisiCalc program specifies conventions for both of these data-entry situations. When you find yourself trying to follow these special conventions, you will sometimes need assurance that you have followed them correctly. The prompt line provides this assurance by telling you whether VisiCalc is accepting your data as a label or a value. We will explore this point in more specific detail later in this chapter.

The third line at the top of your screen is called the edit line. As you enter a label or value into the current position of the work-sheet, the edit line displays the characters that you have typed in so far. If you use the edit command, /E, the editing takes place on the edit line. (Note that this line is currently empty on your spreadsheet, since you haven't entered any data yet.)

Before continuing on to learn about data entry, we should make note of two more pieces of information that are always displayed in the upper right-hand corner of the screen. The first is a letter that indicates the order of calculation; it is initially set at C, for column, but can be changed to R, for row. We'll study the significance of this feature in Chapter 5. The second piece of information, just below the order-of-calculation indicator, is the integer that tells you how much memory remains.

YOUR KEYBOARD

In Chapter 1 we discussed some of the variations that exist between the versions of VisiCalc designed for different personal computers. Your keyboard, which is your only means of communication with the VisiCalc program, may require that you learn its own peculiar combination of keys to perform certain common functions. Using the keyboard will quickly become second-nature to you, once you have learned which keys do what.

In this book we will refer to some keys by names that may or may not correspond exactly to the names of keys on your computer. The *actions* are the same, but the keys that carry out these actions may be different. Here, then, is a list of the names that we will give to the most common keyboard functions:

- The *direction keys: up-arrow, down-arrow, left-arrow, right-arrow*. These are the keys that move the cursor. You may have four distinct keys to move the cursor, or you may have only two. In the latter case, there will be a method of switching the use of the two keys from vertical to horizontal or from horizontal to vertical, and the VisiCalc screen will indicate which direction mode you are in.

- The *escape key*. When you are entering data or using the edit command (/E), this key lets you erase characters from the edit line. Each time you press the escape key, one character is erased.

- The *break key*. This key is valuable in several situations. If you are entering data, recognize a mistake, and wish to erase the entire contents of the edit line, the break key will do it for you. Or, if you are in the middle of executing one of the commands from the command line, and suddenly change your mind, the break key lets you jump completely out of the command, even if you are deeply entrenched in one of the subordinate sets of options. For the break function your computer may have a single key, or you may have to press two keys at once.

- The *return key*. This is the key you use to enter data from the edit line. It may be called ENTER on your keyboard.

Before you read on, you should first find out which keys you have to use on your computer to perform these functions. Appendix C describes these keys for several popular personal computers.

MOVING THE CURSOR . . .
ADJUSTING THE WINDOW

If your VisiCalc screen still looks like Figure 2.1, press the break key to remove the command line from the screen. The cursor is still in the upper-left corner of the worksheet, and the contents line displays the address A1. The prompt line and the edit line are blank.

Let's explore the cursor movements. Press the right-arrow direction key once. Two things happen on your screen: the cursor moves one position to the right, and the contents line shows the address of the new current position, B1. Now press the down-arrow key. The cursor moves down to position B2. Any cursor movement, then, is reflected in two screen details: the actual physical position of the cursor, and the address shown on the contents line.

Now move the cursor over to the far right side of the screen, then down to the bottom right corner of the screen, by pressing the right- and down-arrow keys several times each. Your screen will look something like Figure 2.2 (except, of course, that the address of the lower-right position depends on the number of rows and columns your particular VisiCalc screen displays at a time).

If you press the right-arrow key one more time, you will witness something new: the *window* moves. You know that it has moved

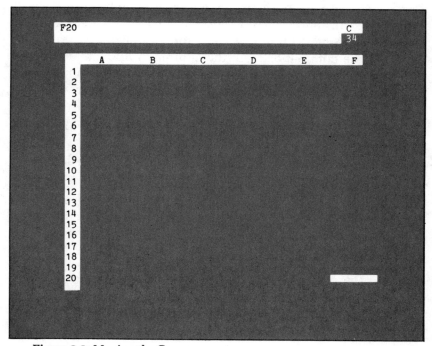

Figure 2.2: Moving the Cursor

because the column labels at the top of the worksheet have shifted one position to the left. Column A is no longer visible, and a new column has moved onto the screen on the right. You can see the same thing happen to the rows if you press the down-arrow key. Row 1 disappears and a new row appears at the bottom of the worksheet. This illustrates the concept of the window. The spreadsheet is large, but the portion of it that you can actually see at one time is limited to the size of your screen. So the VisiCalc program allows you to "move" the screen-window to any portion of the worksheet, by simply moving the cursor. Data that is not currently displayed on the screen is not lost, but simply invisible.

(Actually, you can think of the action on your screen in another way if you like. When the window moves to the right, the spreadsheet *scrolls* to the left, as though both sides of the spreadsheet were wound around turning cylinders. You may hear people refer to either one of these metaphors—either a moving window, or a scrolling spreadsheet. They both mean the same thing.)

Keep moving the cursor to the right. The column labels will go through the entire alphabet, through to Z. Then the columns will be labeled with *two* letters, AA to AZ. But AZ is still not the last column. The next column is BA, and the columns continue on to BK, giving 63 columns in all.

Once you reach column BK, start moving the cursor down. (By the way, your computer may have a *repeat* function to make it easier for you to move the cursor over many positions. There may actually be a repeat key that you press at the same time as the direction key; or, if you hold a direction key down for several seconds, the repeat mode may automatically be activated.) If you keep moving the cursor down, you will eventually reach the actual limit of the VisiCalc spreadsheet. The address of this position is BK254, as shown in Figure 2.3.

A quick multiplication of rows by columns shows that there is a total of just over 16,000 positions on the spreadsheet. Remember, though, that the amount of the spreadsheet that you can actually *use* depends strongly on the amount of memory in your computer.

Now let's move back to position A1. Fortunately the VisiCalc program supplies an instantaneous way of making long cursor jumps over the spreadsheet, so you don't have to move position by position again. This feature is called the *GO TO* command. You use this command by typing the greater-than symbol (>).

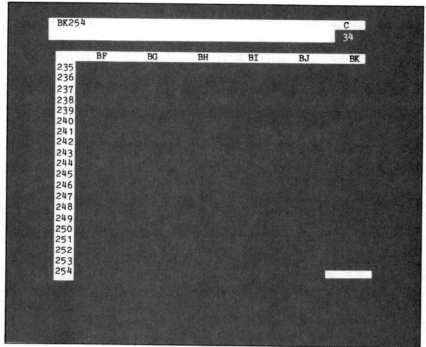

Figure 2.3: The Limits of the Spreadsheet

When you do so, the following message appears on the prompt line:

GO TO: COORDINATE

Coordinate is VisiCalc's word for what we've been calling an address; that is, the column-row identifiers of a position on the spreadsheet. So, the VisiCalc program is waiting for you to type in the address of the position that you want to move to. Type A1; the address will appear on the edit line. Now press the return key, and you will instantly find yourself back in the upper-left corner of the spreadsheet.

You may want to experiment some more with the GO TO command before reading on. To summarize, we have discovered that the VisiCalc spreadsheet has a total of 63 columns (from A to BK) and 254 rows. We can move the cursor to any position by using either the direction keys or the GO TO command. A cursor move to a position outside of the current window will automatically adjust the window also.

ENTERING DATA

There are three different kinds of data entry into the VisiCalc program, but they result in only two different types of data. *Labels* essentially represent nonnumeric data. *Values* and *value references* represent numeric data.

In addition, value references can be used to build *formulas* for your worksheet. Put simply, a value reference is a way of duplicating the contents of any position on your spreadsheet for use in another position.

Let's begin experimenting with the three kinds of input.

LABELS

If your cursor is not at position A1, use the GO TO command to move it there. As an example of label input, begin typing the word VISICALC, and notice what happens at each stage of the input. As soon as you type the first letter, V, four changes occur on the screen:

1. the word LABEL appears on the prompt line, indicating that you are in the process of inputting nonnumeric data;

2. the first letter of input, V, appears in the current position, A1, which is marked by the cursor;

3. the V also appears on the edit line;

4. following the V on the edit line, there will be some graphic representation of a *cue*, indicating that the input is not yet complete. (Again, the shape of this cue depends on your version of the VisiCalc program. It may be a flashing square, or simply an underscore character.) As long as this cue is displayed, you know that you still have the option of cancelling the input by pressing the break key, or erasing the previous character by pressing the escape key.

So, to freeze a moment in time, here is what the top three lines of the screen look like after you have typed the V of VISICALC:

A1

LABEL

V☐

Continue typing the word. Each time you type a letter, the character appears at both the cursor position and the edit line, and the cue at the edit line moves one space to the right. When you have typed the entire word, press the return key, and watch what happens. Both the prompt line and the edit line go blank, telling you that you have completed the input operation. The word VISICALC remains in position A1. And, as long as the cursor also remains at A1, the contents line displays the following information:

    A1 (L) VISICALC

This tells you that position A1 contains a label (the significance of the L in parentheses), specifically the word "VISICALC".

Now press the right-arrow key to move the cursor to position B1. The contents line now displays the new position of the cursor—B1—but position A1 of the spreadsheet still contains the label that you typed into it.

Let's see what happens when we move the *window* to the right. Press the right-arrow key several times, until column A moves outside of the window. Now you can no longer see the word that you entered into position A1, but it's still there. To convince yourself, use the GO TO command to return to A1, and you will find the word VISICALC, just as it was when you left it.

VALUES

Move the cursor to position B1 now, and type a number, say 1983. Notice the display on the three information lines before you press the return key:

    B1
    VALUE
    1983☐

The prompt line tells you that you've typed a value, and the edit line displays the value. Nothing is displayed yet in position B1 itself, though, until you press the return key to enter the value. Go ahead and press the return key now to see what happens. The number will appear at position B1, and the prompt line and edit line will clear. The contents line now displays the new value of position B1:

    B1 (V) 1983

The V in parentheses tells you that B1 contains a value.

With both a label and a value now on the screen, you may notice an interesting detail about the way the VisiCalc program displays the two different types of information. Labels are automatically left-justified, and values are automatically right-justified. This means that the V of the word VISICALC appears in the very first space of position A1, but the 3 in 1983 appears in the very last space of position B1. This way of presenting data corresponds with the way we usually prepare tables. We tend to align columns of words on the left and numbers on the right.

VALUE REFERENCES

Finally, we come to value references, the third, and most versatile kind of data entry. A value reference is a way of telling the VisiCalc program to access and repeat a value from a specified position on the spreadsheet. Value references can be used in several ways in the VisiCalc program, as we will see in this chapter and the next. For now, we'll just take a quick first look at the meaning and use of value references.

Move the cursor to position C1, directly to the right of the value you just entered. We are going to type the *address* of that previous value into C1; as a result, we will see the value itself transferred to C1.

To enter a value reference, we must first tell the VisiCalc program that a value entry, not a label entry, is coming up. If we were to type the address "B1" into a position, VisiCalc would read it as a label, because B, the first character, is nonnumeric. The correct way to enter the value reference, then, is to begin the address with a plus sign (+). In addition to the digits 0 to 9, the VisiCalc program reads several other characters as "flags" for numeric data entry. Among these are the plus sign, the minus sign, the decimal point, and the left parenthesis.

So let's try it. Type +B1; the following information will appear on the top three lines of the screen:

```
C1
VALUE
+B1□
```

Thanks to the plus sign, VisiCalc has, indeed, recognized the address B1 as a value. Now press the return key and see what happens. The contents line shows the value reference that you typed into C1:

    C1 (V) +B1

But the position on the spreadsheet itself shows the value, 1983. In other words, by entering a value reference into position C1, you have instructed the VisiCalc program to give C1 the same value as is contained in B1.

Now if you move the cursor back to B1 and enter a new value, you will see that the value of C1 also changes. The value of C1 depends entirely on the contents of position B1. For example, if you enter 1984 into B1, you will see the same new value appear in position C1.

EDITING DATA—THE /E COMMAND

Now that we've learned some of the fundamentals of data entry in the VisiCalc program, it's time to start working with the VisiCalc commands. The first one we'll look at is the edit command.

You'll recall that pressing the slash key displays the commands on the prompt line. Move the cursor to position A1, where the word VISICALC is still displayed, and type the slash. Look at your command line to see if you have the letter E, for edit. If you don't see an E, then your version of VisiCalc doesn't have the edit feature. (Don't worry—the /E command is a convenience, but not an essential part of the VisiCalc program.) If your command line does include an E, then type E on the keyboard. Here's what you'll see on the top three lines of the screen:

    A1 (L) VISICALC
    [EDIT]: LABEL
    ⊠ISICALC

The prompt line shows you that you are ready to edit the label contents of position A1. The edit line displays the label, with a cue marking the edit position. You can do one of several things at this point:

- use the left- or right-arrow key to move the edit cue over any position on the edit line;

- type any character that you wish to *insert* into the contents of the position (the cue marks the positions where the character will be inserted);

- type the escape key to delete the character that is immediately to the left of the edit cue;
- type the return key to enter the new edited data into the current position;
- type the break key to cancel the edit command; the original contents of the position will remain unchanged.

Just to experiment with the edit command, we'll change the word VISICALC to VISIBLE. Type the right-arrow key eight times, to position the edit cue at the end of the word. Then type the escape key four times; this will delete the last four letters of the word. Finally, type the letters BLE, and then the return key. The new contents of A1 should be the word VISIBLE.

You might want to practice using the edit command now before continuing on. This command will prove to be useful later when you begin to type formulas into your worksheet.

If you don't have the edit command, do not despair. You can achieve the same results by simply retyping the desired new contents of a position. In the case of formulas this may take a little longer than using the edit command would, but it is just as reliable.

CLEAR THE SCREEN AND START OVER...

The next command we will learn is a convenient but dangerous one. The /C command gives you a clean slate, an empty VisiCalc screen, to work with. You can use it any time you want to clear away old data, mistaken formulas, or information that you just don't want to deal with today, thank you. Three quick keystrokes, and you start from scratch. That's the convenient part.

The dangerous part is that you'll never see that data again unless you've saved it first on disk. So far in this chapter we haven't typed in anything worth saving, so we can be fairly cavalier about learning to use the /C command. But in the future you'll have to use /C with caution.

So, type /C. Notice that when you have typed the slash, you don't necessarily have to pause to look at the command line before you invoke one of the commands. As you become more and more familiar with the VisiCalc features you will seldom need to look at the command line at all.

The clear command produces the following message on the prompt line:

CLEAR: TYPE Y TO CONFIRM

This is your chance to change your mind. Type anything but the letter Y and the command will be cancelled. But if you're sure that you have nothing to lose (which is the case at the moment), type Y and watch the results. Your entire screen will go blank for a moment and then the VisiCalc program will come back, as though you had just loaded it from the disk.

This is perhaps a good time to point out the copyright and version information. When you first load the VisiCalc program, or when you use the clear command, the prompt line and the edit line initially have the program's copyright notice and the identification numbers of the particular version of the program that you are using. (You may need the latter information for inquiries to the manufacturer.) You can also access this information at any time during a session with the VisiCalc program, by using the version command. Just type /V.

With a clear screen in front of us, we are now going to type in a column of numbers, to prepare for the next section of this chapter. We'll be using the first column of numbers from the table in Figure 1.1. Here are the numbers:

```
11.18
 7.62
11.18
 1.52
 4.83
11.43
 6.6
 5.59
 6.6
 6.86
```

Notice that most of the numbers have two digits after the decimal point, but a couple of them have only one. You should type them exactly as you see them here, because we'll use this inconsistency to illustrate a VisiCalc feature.

Here is one more useful point about inputting rows or columns of data. After typing a number, you may enter it by pressing a direction key rather than the return key, if you wish. The advantage of this feature is one of speed when you have lots of numbers to type in. With a single keystroke, you accomplish two tasks: the data entry, and the cursor movement.

For example, type the first number in the list, 11.18, into position A1. Now press the down-arrow key and notice what happens. The value, 11.18, is stored in position A1, and the cursor is at position A2, ready for you to enter the next value of the column.

Finish entering the rest of the numbers, then type >A1 to reposition the cursor. Your worksheet should look like Figure 2.4.

Figure 2.4: First Column of Numbers

CONTROLLING THE SPREADSHEET

Recall that in Chapter 1 we informally classified the VisiCalc commands into three functional groups: calculation, control, and storage. We're just about ready to begin using a few of the commands that control the spreadsheet. Before we do, though, we should discuss some matters of notation. You may have noticed in the previous paragraph that you were instructed to type >A1 instead of "type the GO TO command to place the cursor at A1." This is representative of a kind of shorthand notation that we can use to describe a detailed sequence of commands on the VisiCalc program. There is no *standard* way to write down all the commands; to a certain extent you can devise any notation you choose, as long as you and others can quickly understand what the command is that you've written. Here are a few examples of notation that you'll soon begin seeing in this book:

/CY (invoke the clear command, and confirm the action by typing Y)

/GF$(choose the dollar-and-cent option of the global for-
    mat command)
/TV (establish a column of fixed titles)

Don't worry for the moment about the meaning of the latter two
commands; we'll be studying them shortly. But consider the advantages of this notation. After every part of a multiple-character
command, the VisiCalc program displays your next options on
the prompt line. Beginners tend to type commands in slowly, con-
sulting the prompt line carefully at each stage of the process. (We
will do the same in this chapter, as we examine each command
prompt for the first time.) As you get used to the commands,
though, you'll barely hesitate when you type in a long command
like /GF$. When you reach this point, the shorthand notation will
tend to make more sense; you'll begin thinking of a four-character
command combination as what it really is—a single command to
perform one desired action.

Let's return to our column of numbers. The first two actions
we'll take are both global command options. Global means that
the command affects the entire worksheet. Type /G to see the four
options that the global command offers you. Here is what you'll
see on the prompt line:

GLOBAL: C O R F

The middle two options, O and R, involve calculation on your
spreadsheet. We'll ignore them for the moment. The two that concern us now are C (for column width) and F (for format).

The /GC command allows you to change the width (i.e., the
number of spaces) of the columns on your spreadsheet. The
VisiCalc program starts you out with 9 spaces per column. You
may decrease the width to as few as 3 spaces, or increase it to as
many spaces as you need, up to the maximum screen width. It is
to your advantage to adjust the column width of your worksheet
down to as few spaces as you anticipate you'll need. This allows
you to see more columns on your screen at a time.

For this example, we're going to decrease the width of the columns to 7 spaces. To choose the C option of the global command,
you simply type C in response to the display of the global options
on the prompt line. The following line will appear next on the
prompt line:

COLUMN WIDTH

Respond by typing a 7 and the return key, then watch the action on your screen. All the columns are instantly reorganized in a smaller width, and an extra column or two will appear on the right side of the screen.

Next we'll use a global format command to align the decimal points of the column of numbers. All numbers will be displayed with two digits after the decimal point after we use this command.

Type the global format command, /GF. On the prompt line you'll see the seven options offered by this command:

FORMAT: D G I L R $ *

These options change the *display* of data on the screen. The format commands do *not*, however, change the computer's *memory* of the contents of a position. This is an important distinction. What you *see* in any given position may not be exactly the same as the value that is actually stored in that position.

The global format command, /GF, and the format command, /F, both offer the same options. The difference is that /GF affects *all* the positions of the spreadsheet, whereas /F works only on the current cursor position. Briefly, here is what the options do: The I, $, and * options change the format of *values* to integer, dollar-and-cent, and bar-graph displays, respectively. The R and L options are for right- and left-justification of both values and labels. (For left-justified values, a leading blank is maintained before each value so that numbers won't run into each other.) The G option changes values and labels to their *general* format—the format that the spreadsheet is in when you first start the VisiCalc program. The general format displays:

- left-justified labels with as many characters as will fit in the current column width;

- right-justified numbers, always with a leading blank maintained before the value.

Finally, the /FD command *defaults* an individual position to the current global format. (The /GFD command has no effect at all on the spreadsheet display.)

We'll see many examples of these commands in this chapter and the chapters ahead. The format option that we are interested in now is the global dollar-and-cent option, /GF$. Type the $ key and notice what happens. The two numbers that previously had only one digit after the decimal point are now filled out with zeros, so that their decimal points align with the rest of the column. Your screen should now look like Figure 2.5. Move the cursor to position A9 to examine one of the numbers that changed. On the spreadsheet itself, the number should be displayed as 6.60. But look at the contents line, at the top of the screen:

A9 (V) 6.6

The actual contents of the position are unchanged; only the display on the spreadsheet has been reformatted.

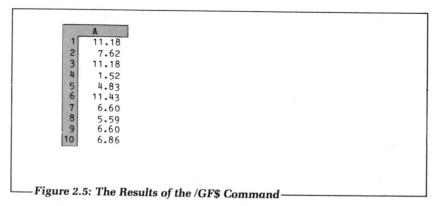

Figure 2.5: The Results of the /GF$ Command

Let's explore a little deeper into the dollar-and-cent formatting. Remember, you used a *global* command for this format. This means that any number you type onto the spreadsheet, no matter how you enter it in, will be displayed with two digits after the decimal point. Try it. Move the cursor down to an empty position below the column of numbers, say position A15. First enter an integer—2. On the spreadsheet it will appear as 2.00. Now move down to position A16 and enter the number 3.246. The number will be displayed as 3.25. This shows you yet another feature of the /GF$ command. Numbers with more than two digits after the decimal point are *rounded* for display. But again, notice the contents line:

A16 (V) 3.246

Try one more number. Move to A17 and enter the number 123456. The resulting spreadsheet display might be somewhat of a surprise to you. In the dollar-and-cent format you would expect the number to be displayed as 123456.00. But remember that the width of your columns is only 7 spaces, not enough to display this number. VisiCalc's way of telling you that this can't be displayed is to fill position A17 with a row of greater-than symbols:

>>>>>>

The contents line shows, however, that the number is actually stored in the position, even though you can't see it there on the spreadsheet:

A17 (V) 123456

While we're experimenting, we should try one more thing. You have seen what happens when you try to enter a *number* that is too big for the column width of the spreadsheet. Now let's see what happens in the case of a label. Move the cursor to position A18 and type the word VISICALC. When you entered this word earlier in this chapter, the columns were 9 spaces wide; now they are only 7. Notice what happens when you enter the word now. The contents line shows the entire word, as you would expect:

A18 (L) VISICALC

But the position itself only has room for the first 7 characters, so that's all you get:

VISICAL

The numbers we have typed into positions A15, A16, and A17, and the label in position A18 were for experimentation only. We don't want them to remain as part of our worksheet. How do we get rid of them? Obviously the /C command is not what we want at this point, because we would lose the column of numbers. Rather, this is a job for the blank command.

Make sure the cursor is positioned at one of the four entries that you want to erase. Then type /B for the blank command. The prompt line will simply say:

BLANK

To carry out the blank command you must type the return key at this point, and the value in the current position will disappear. Then do the same with the other entries.

Now type >A1 to move the cursor back up to the upper-left corner of the spreadsheet. We are ready to start supplying some meaning to these numbers, and of course the way to do this is to type in some labels. We're going to add the names of the sales-people from Figure 1.3:

BAKER
SMITH
FLINT
BROWN
VERN
MARLOW
HARPER
FLEMING
NASH
WHITE

We'd like to put them in a column just to the left of the numbers; in other words, we want the names to become column A and the numbers to move to column B. Unfortunately we didn't think ahead to leave room for the column of labels.

The VisiCalc program solves this problem with the insert com-mand. Type the command /I. The prompt line tells you that you may insert either a row or a column:

INSERT: R C

At the moment you want an extra column, so type C. Keep your eye on the screen, or you'll miss the action. The column of numbers will slide swiftly over one column to the right, leaving column A empty. Now you're ready to input the names of the ten salespeople. Remember to use the down-arrow key, rather than the return key after you type each name. When all the names are entered, your spreadsheet will look like Figure 2.6.

When you start preparing large spreadsheets, you'll frequently want a way to keep a row or column of labels on the screen when you move the window. For example, say you have a table of twelve columns of numbers (as you will, eventually, for your salespeople in this spreadsheet). To see the last columns on the right you have to move the window over, but you still want to keep the column of labels in view for reference. The VisiCalc titles command is the feature that arranges this for you.

Move the cursor to position A1 and type /T to see the titles option:

TITLES: H V B N

	A	B
1	BAKER	11.18
2	SMITH	7.62
3	FLINT	11.18
4	BROWN	1.52
5	VERN	4.83
6	MARLOW	11.43
7	HARPER	6.60
8	FLEMING	5.59
9	NASH	6.60
10	WHITE	6.86

Figure 2.6: Adding a Column of Names to the Spreadsheet

H stands for horizontal, and V for vertical. These two options allow you to establish either a row or column of fixed titles. B, for both, establishes both a row *and* a column of titles at once. For example, if the cursor is at position A1, and you want column A and row 1 both to be fixed as titles, then you simply type /TB.

In our current example, we want to set the column of salespeople's names as fixed titles; so type V. Now move the cursor into column B, and then try to move it back into column A again. You can't do it; the column is fixed.

To see what happens when the window shifts, move the cursor several columns to the right. When the window moves, you lose column B, but column A stays on the screen.

There *is* a way to position the cursor inside a fixed row or column if you need to make a change in one of the entries. You have to use the GO TO command. Try it by typing >A1.

Finally, the /T command offers one last option that we haven't discussed yet—the N option. If you want to return to unfixed titles, use /TN. The N stands for none.

So far, then, we have two columns of information on our spreadsheet, a column of names and a column of numbers. Recall from Chapter 1 that the numbers represent sales, in units of a thousand dollars, for each salesperson during one month. We have formatted the entire screen for dollar-and-cent numerical data (/GF$), and we have decreased the width of the columns to 7 spaces (/GC7). We have also used the insert command (/I), the blank command (/B) and the titles command (/T). In the next sections we'll begin writing—and then replicating—formulas on our worksheet.

WRITING FORMULAS

In our salesperson example we said that the monthly salaries would be calculated from a base salary of $1000, plus a 5% commission on sales. We could write this as:

salary = $1000 + (.05 × sales)

Thus, given the monthly sales for each salesperson, we could easily calculate the salaries. To write this formula on the VisiCalc spreadsheet, we will make use of what we have learned about *value references*.

To start out, let's look at the first salesperson on the list—Baker. The sales figure for Baker, at position B1, is 11.18, meaning total sales of $11,180 for the month. What we want to do, then, to find Baker's salary is multiply 11.18 by .05 (to find the commission) and add 1 (representing $1000 base salary). We will carry out this calculation in a VisiCalc *formula*.

To create formulas for the spreadsheet, the VisiCalc program allows us to perform the *arithmetic operations* (addition, subtraction, multiplication, division, and exponentiation) on value references. The symbols we use to write these formulas are:

+   addition
−   subtraction
*   multiplication
/   division
^   exponentiation

To find Baker's salary, then, all we need to do is write the appropriate formula using a value reference to position B1 for the sales figure. The elements of our formula will look something like this:

1+.05*B1

In other words, we want to multiply the contents of position B1 by .05 and then add 1.

However, another important consideration enters into the problem—the *order of operations*. Normally, in algebraic statements, or in most programming languages, the standard convention is that multiplication and division are performed *before* addition and subtraction, no matter what order the expression is actually *written* in. This, of course, makes a big difference in formulas like the one above. Adding 1 to .05 and then multiplying the sum by the sales figure would result in a very inaccurate salary result. (Good for the salesperson, but bad for the company.)

The VisiCalc program, as it turns out, does *not* follow the convention of performing multiplication and division first. Instead, VisiCalc performs operations *in the order that they are written in the formula itself*. This is inevitably a source of confusion when you first start writing formulas on your spreadsheets. The VisiCalc program does, however, provide a means of *changing* the order of calculation if you need to. That is by using *parentheses* in formulas. Expressions within parentheses are calculated first. For example, in the salary formula, where we definitely want the multiplication to be performed before the addition, we can include a set of parentheses around the multiplication expression, and the formula will be calculated correctly:

$1 + (.05 * B1)$

Another way of handling the formula, of course, would be to reverse the order of operations:

$.05 * B1 + 1$

In this case the parentheses are not necessary because the VisiCalc program will automatically perform the multiplication first. Even so, it is a good practice to include parentheses, even when they are not absolutely necessary:

$(.05 * B1) + 1$

If you get into this habit, it will save you serious trouble when you start writing long and complicated formulas.

Let's enter the formula now and see what the result will be. Column C is going to be our salary column, so move the cursor to position C1. Begin typing the formula:

$1 + (.05 * \square$

You'll notice that the VALUE indicator is displayed on the prompt line, and your formula appears character-by-character on the edit line. When you reach the point where you are ready to enter the value reference—B1—you have a choice of methods. You can, if you want, simply type the characters in the normal way, complete the formula, and press the return key. However, in

many situations, when both your formulas and your spreadsheets get long and detailed, you may not know the exact address
of the position that you want to use as a value reference. You may
be in the middle of writing a formula and suddenly realize that the
value you want to reference is not even showing in your current
window. It would be terribly inconvenient to have to abandon the
formula you'd begun, search around the spreadsheet for the position that contains the value you want to reference, and then
return to rewrite the formula.

Fortunately, the VisiCalc program saves you from this inconve-
nience. You can move the cursor around the spreadsheet *during
the process of entering a formula*, as long as you have reached a
point in the formula where a value reference is appropriate. The
current position of your cursor will be displayed on the edit line
as the value reference.

Let's see how this works. So far you have typed:

    1+(.05∗ □

The edit cue is indicating that the VisiCalc program is waiting for
you to complete your formula. The cursor is at position C1. Press
the left-arrow direction key to move the cursor to B1, and watch
what happens on the edit line. The value reference, B1, appears
automatically as part of your formula:

    1+(.05∗B1 □

Since B1 is the value reference you want, you can now type the
right-parenthesis character to complete your formula. Two things
happen. The character appears on the edit line, so that you now
have:

    1+(.05∗B1)□

And, the cursor returns to position C1.

Press the return key to see the result of the formula. Baker's salary
for the month is expressed as 1.56 (meaning, of course, $1,560).

To summarize, there are two essential things to remember
when you enter formulas that contain value references. First, you
can enter the value reference itself either by typing it in manually,
or by moving the cursor to the actual position that you wish to
reference. Second, the VisiCalc program performs operations in
the order that you write them, unless you include parentheses
in your formula.

REPLICATING FORMULAS

We've now calculated Baker's salary, but we still have the rest of the salespeople to deal with. Of course, one thing we could do is simply retype the salary formula once for each salesperson. That would produce the results, but would take a long time, and may lead to errors.

The replication command (/R) is designed for just this kind of situation. You have written a formula, and you would like to *apply* the formula to many pieces of data without having to retype the formula each time.

To watch the replication command in action, make sure the cursor is still located at position C1, and type /R. The prompt line will display the message:

REPLICATE: SOURCE RANGE OR RETURN

and the edit line will appear as:

C1 □

The replication command goes through three phases of instructions before actually carrying out its task. In the first phase, you must indicate which formulas you want to replicate. This is called the *source range*. In this example you are only going to replicate a single formula—the one that calculates salaries—but later you'll be replicating several formulas at once. The source range phase of the replication command is designed to handle both of these situations. For now, to indicate that the formula at C1 is the only formula you want to replicate, simply type the return key. The edit line will automatically display the source range of a single formula:

C1...C1: □

The prompt line displays a new message:

REPLICATE: TARGET RANGE

This is the second phase of the replication command. You must now indicate the range over which you want to apply the formula at C1. The target range will appear on the edit line in the same format as the source range:

position...position

Just as with formula value references, you have the option of *typing* the addresses of the two positions, or moving the cursor to the position that you want to indicate as part of the range.

To complete column C, then, with the salaries for each of the salespeople, your target range will be position C2 to position C10. Type the first address, C2, then type a period. Your edit line will now look like this:

>   C1...C1: C2... □

Notice that you only have to type the period once, but it results in three periods on the edit line. Now type C10 and the return key. This will put you into the third, and perhaps most complex, stage of the replication command.

In order to carry out the replication, the VisiCalc program now needs to know how to treat any value references that appear in the formula. Are the value references to be treated as constants or variables? Should the VisiCalc program use the same value each time it replicates the formula, or should it go down the corresponding column (or across the corresponding row) and change the value reference for each replication?

Look at the prompt line to see how VisiCalc asks this question:

>   REPLICATE: N=NO CHANGE, R=RELATIVE

The edit line now shows your formula, with the edit cue positioned at the value reference:

>   C1: C2...C10: 1+(.05* B1

You answer the prompt by typing an N or an R for each value reference of the formula. In this instance there is only one value reference, B1. Do you want to use B1 (i.e., Baker's sales) in each of the applications of the salary formula, or do you want to use each corresponding value from column B (B2, B3, B4, and so on)? Clearly the latter. So, you simply type R, for relative.

Since this is the only value reference, you instantly get a column of numbers that represent the salaries for each salesperson. Your spreadsheet should now look like Figure 2.7.

We have worked through the three phases of the replication command in a fairly easy example. In the next section we will increase the value of our worksheet by *generalizing* the salary formula.

```
        A        B        C
   1 BAKER    11.18     1.56
   2 SMITH     7.62     1.38
   3 FLINT    11.18     1.56
   4 BROWN     1.52     1.08
   5 VERN      4.83     1.24
   6 MARLOW   11.43     1.57
   7 HARPER    6.60     1.33
   8 FLEMING   5.59     1.28
   9 NASH      6.60     1.33
  10 WHITE     6.86     1.34
```

Figure 2.7: The Replicated Salary Formula

MORE ON REPLICATION

Let's say you are thinking of changing the base salary and commission rate for your salespeople. You believe that your present salary does not provide enough incentive for your best salespeople. You'd like to have a quick way of examining what would happen to gross salaries under several revised salary-plus-commission plans.

In the previous version of your spreadsheet you wrote the base salary and the commission rates directly into the salary formula as constants. That method produced the correct results, but is not very convenient for your present need to try out other values.

A better, more generalized, approach is to write a formula in which the base salary and commission rate are *value references* in your formula rather than constants. You can then easily change these values and examine how the change affects actual salaries. Let's see how this method works.

First, we may as well delete the current version of column C, since we're going to revise it completely. The delete command allows us to delete a row or a column of information. Move the cursor to position C1 and type /D to invoke the command. On the prompt line you will see:

    DELETE: R C

Type C to delete the column.

Now we have to specify two convenient positions somewhere on the spreadsheet for the base salary and the commission rate. Let's store them in B12 and B13, respectively. We'll begin with the original salary schedule. Type >B12, and enter the value 1 (representing $1,000); then enter .05 (for 5%) in position B13.

Our new salary formula, then, will contain value references to B12 and B13, rather than the constants 1 and .05. Move the cursor back up to C1, and type in the following formula:

+B12+(B13*B1)

(Do you recall why the formula must begin with a plus sign?) Hit the return key, and the value 1.56 should appear in position C1—the same value produced by the previous formula.

Now we must replicate the new formula for the entire group of salespeople. Respond to the first two phases of the replication command in the same way you did before—press the return key for the source range (indicating that C1 is the only formula) and type C2.C10 and the return key to produce the target range.

The third phase requires more careful analysis. The base salary and the commission rate remain constant for each salesperson, but the sales figures will vary in each case. So you'll have to type two N's (no change) for B12 and B13, and an R (relative) for B1. Notice the action on the edit line during this phase. The VisiCalc program poses the edit cue over each value reference in turn, and stops to let you consider how the reference should be treated. Here is what the sequence of edit cues will look like; first, the cue for B12:

C1: C2...C10: + B12

You type an N, and then the cue for B13 appears:

C1: C2...C10: +B12+(B13

Again you type an N, and the last cue appears:

C1: C2...C10: +B12+(B13* B1

Finally, you type an R to indicate that the reference to B1 should be treated as a variable.

When the replication is complete, column C on your worksheet should have the same values as before. Look back at Figure 2.7 and compare.

The difference between the two versions of the formula is this: you can now change the base salary and the commission and instantly see the resulting change in the salary column.

For example, let's say you are considering decreasing the base salary to $500, but increasing the commission to 10%. All you have to do is change the values in positions B12 and B13, and watch the new results in column C.

Try it. Move the cursor to B12 and enter the new value .5 (for $500). Then enter .1 (for 10%) in B13. Each time you change one of these values, the VisiCalc program *recalculates* the formulas that are dependent on these values—that is, positions C1 to C10. Your new worksheet (at $500 and 10%) should look like Figure 2.8. Notice the result of the new salary schedule: the best salespeople would see an increase in total salary, but the weaker salespeople would take a cut in salary.

	A	B	C
1	BAKER	11.18	1.62
2	SMITH	7.62	1.26
3	FLINT	11.18	1.62
4	BROWN	1.52	0.65
5	VERN	4.83	0.98
6	MARLOW	11.43	1.64
7	HARPER	6.60	1.16
8	FLEMING	5.59	1.06
9	NASH	6.60	1.16
10	WHITE	6.86	1.19
11			
12		0.50	
13		0.10	

Figure 2.8:
Generalized Salary Formula (Base Salary of $500 and 10% Commission)

In Chapter 5 we will further explore this method of generalizing the use of formulas in the VisiCalc program. This is what VisiCalc users mean when they talk about exploring "what-if" scenarios. What will happen if you change the salary schedule? What if one of your salespeople manages to increase monthly sales by 50%? You can see the answers to these questions quickly and easily using the VisiCalc program.

WINDOWS AND GRAPHICS

We'll be expanding the worksheet considerably in the next chapters; but before we move on, let's embellish this current version a bit. Specifically, in this section we'll add some column headings, split the window, and create a bar graph.

Begin by using the insert command to create two empty rows at the top of the spreadsheet. Position the cursor in row 1, and type /IR twice. The sales table will move down to rows 3 to 12. Now move the cursor to position A1. (You'll have to use the GO TO command. Remember why?) Enter the label NAME. Then enter SALES and SALARY in B1 and C1, respectively. To make these latter two labels correspond more clearly to the right-justified columns of the numbers they head, you may want to reformat them. You can use the /FR command to right-justify a label. Simply type the command while the cursor is located in the target position.

Now move the cursor to A2 (again using the GO TO command, since column A is fixed as a title-column). We're going to draw a double line (actually made up of a row of equal signs) between the column headings and the table itself. To do so, we use the repeating label command, /−. When you type the command you'll see the following message appear on the prompt line:

LABEL: REPEATING

You may enter any character or series of characters that you want to be repeated in the position. Type the equal sign (=) and then press return. Seven equal signs will appear in position A2:

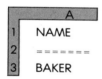

Notice how the contents line describes this entry:

A2 (/−) =

Even if you should decide later to increase or decrease the width of your columns, the repeating character (= in this case) will always fill the position.

A repeating label can be replicated. With the cursor at position A2, use the /R command to replicate the label over the positions B2 to C2. Figure 2.9 shows what your worksheet should look like now.

Next we'll add a second window to the VisiCalc screen. There are actually several reasons why you might want to have two windows to view your worksheet. One of these reasons, which we have already mentioned, is to view two distant parts of your worksheet at the same time. Another, perhaps less obvious, reason is to create two *differently formatted* views of the worksheet. When you have two windows, you can give each one

```
          A       B       C
     1 NAME    SALES  SALARY
     2 =======================
     3 BAKER    11.18    1.62
     4 SMITH     7.62    1.26
     5 FLINT    11.18    1.62
     6 BROWN     1.52    0.65
     7 VERN      4.83    0.98
     8 MARLOW   11.43    1.64
     9 HARPER    6.60    1.16
    10 FLEMING   5.59    1.06
    11 NASH      6.60    1.16
    12 WHITE     6.86    1.19
    13
    14           0.50
    15           0.10
```

Figure 2.9: Sales Table with Column Headings

different global formats, fixed titles, and column widths. That's what we're going to do with our worksheet now.

Put your cursor at position D1, and type the window command, /W. Here's the prompt you'll see:

WINDOW: H V 1 S U

H and V are for horizontal and vertical window splits, respectively. You can create windows in either direction. The 1 option is to return to a single-window screen. (The S and U options are for synchronized or unsynchronized movement of the two windows.)

We're going to create a vertical split at column D, so type V. Now you have a window on the right and a window on the left. The cursor can only be displayed in one window at a time. To move the cursor back and forth between windows, simply press the semicolon key (;). Try it several times to see how it works. Then put the cursor in the new window on the right.

When you create a new window, it takes on all the format characteristics of the original single window. Notice that the window on the right has columns that are 7 characters wide, a fixed column of titles (column A), and a global dollar-and-cent format. We want to change all of these characteristics now.

First, to get rid of the fixed titles, type /TN (for *no* titles). Next, increase the column width of the window on the right by typing /GC13. Notice that neither of these changes affects the window on the left.

Now put the cursor at position B1 in the window on the right.

You'll see the same column of sales figures as on the left, only right-justified in a much wider column. To provide a visual representation of the sales figures, it would be nice to create a bar graph. Remarkably enough, we can do so with a single VisiCalc command. The * option of the global format command converts numbers into rows of asterisks. For example, the number 10 transforms into ten asterisks. The command doesn't affect labels.

Be prepared for a pleasant surprise when you type the command: /GF*. Column B is instantly transformed into a bar graph of sales. You can see now why we increased the width of the column—to accomodate the entire length of the bar graph. Your spreadsheet should now look like Figure 2.10.

	A	B	C		B
1	NAME	SALES	SALARY	1	SALES
2	=====================			2	==============
3	BAKER	11.18	1.62	3	**********
4	SMITH	7.62	1.26	4	*******
5	FLINT	11.18	1.62	5	**********
6	BROWN	1.52	0.65	6	*
7	VERN	4.83	0.98	7	****
8	MARLOW	11.43	1.64	8	***********
9	HARPER	6.60	1.16	9	*****
10	FLEMING	5.59	1.06	10	*****
11	NASH	6.60	1.16	11	*****
12	WHITE	6.86	1.19	12	*****
13				13	
14		0.50		14	
15		0.10		15	

Figure 2.10: A Second Window for the Bar Graph

STORING SPREADSHEETS—/SS AND /SL

When you've worked hard to create a spreadsheet, you will of course want to save it on disk so you can refer to it or revise it at a later date. The storage command, /S, is the feature that allows you to do so. You can also *load* a VisiCalc file back into the memory of the computer; *delete* a file from the disk; *initialize* a disk so that you can use it for storage; *quit* the VisiCalc program; or store a DIF file—all this with the /S command.

Type the command, and you will see the options that correspond to these functions:

    STORAGE: L S D I Q #

Make sure you have a properly initialized disk in your disk drive. (If necessary, use the /SI command to initialize a brand new disk.) Type the S option of the storage command to save your spreadsheet. The prompt line will display the message:

STORAGE: FILE FOR SAVING

and the edit cue will appear, waiting for you to type a file name. You might decide to call this particular file something like SALES.

Since the VisiCalc program lets you save more than one kind of file on disk, it is a good idea to include extensions for your file names. For example, SALES.VC would be for a VisiCalc spreadsheet file, and SALES.DIF for a DIF file. (Some versions of the program automatically include these extensions for you.)

Once you've typed a file name, press the return key, and the file will be saved. Now you can clear your spreadsheet (/CY) and try *loading* the same file back into VisiCalc from the disk. Type /SL, and again the prompt line asks you for a file name, but this time it will be the name of the file you want to load:

STORAGE: FILE TO LOAD

You may simply type the file name, SALES.VC, and then press return. But what if you don't remember the names of all the files you have on disk? How can you get a list of the names of the files? The answer: simply press the right-arrow key instead of typing a name. The VisiCalc program will access the disk, and display (on the edit line) the name of the first file. For example:

STORAGE: FILE TO LOAD
SALES.VC□

Notice the edit cue waiting for your response. If you type the return key at this point, then VisiCalc will load the file SALES.VC. Later on, after you have stored several files on the disk, you can use the right-arrow key to display the names of all your files, one by one. You can go through the entire list of files (called the disk *directory*) this way, or you can choose to load one of the files by pressing the return key.

Load SALES.VC to make sure the save operation worked properly. The spreadsheet should look just like it did before (see Figure 2.10).

SUMMARY

The three kinds of data entry into the VisiCalc program result in two types of data. Values are numerical data; labels are non-numerical. Value references, which are the building blocks of formulas, result in numerical values.

We have divided the VisiCalc commands into three categories. The control commands that we have seen up to now include:

/B	(to erase the contents of a position)
/CY	(to clear the entire screen)
/D	(to delete a row or column)
/E	(to edit the contents of a position)
/GC	(to change the column width)
/GF$	(to format dollar-and-cent numerical data)
/GF*	(to create bar graphs out of numerical data)
/I	(to insert a row or a column)
/T	(to fix titles)
/W	(to create a second window)

The format commands change only the *display* of data, not the actual memory contents of a position. Split windows may be used either to view two different parts of a spreadsheet, or to view a single part in two different formats.

The replication command applies a formula over a range of positions. The command guides you through three phases: you must specify the source range of formulas, and the target range of positions. Finally, you must indicate whether each value reference in the formula is a constant (no change) or a variable (relative).

You can often generalize formulas—and examine "what-if" scenarios—by writing them in terms of value references, rather than explicit numbers.

The versatile /S command provides for several kinds of storage and retrieval of disk files.

CHAPTER THREE

VISICALC FUNCTIONS (PART I)

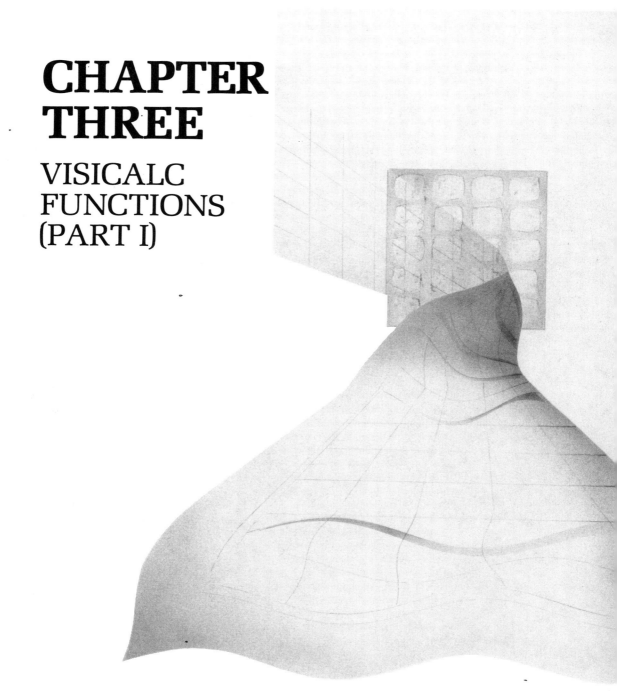

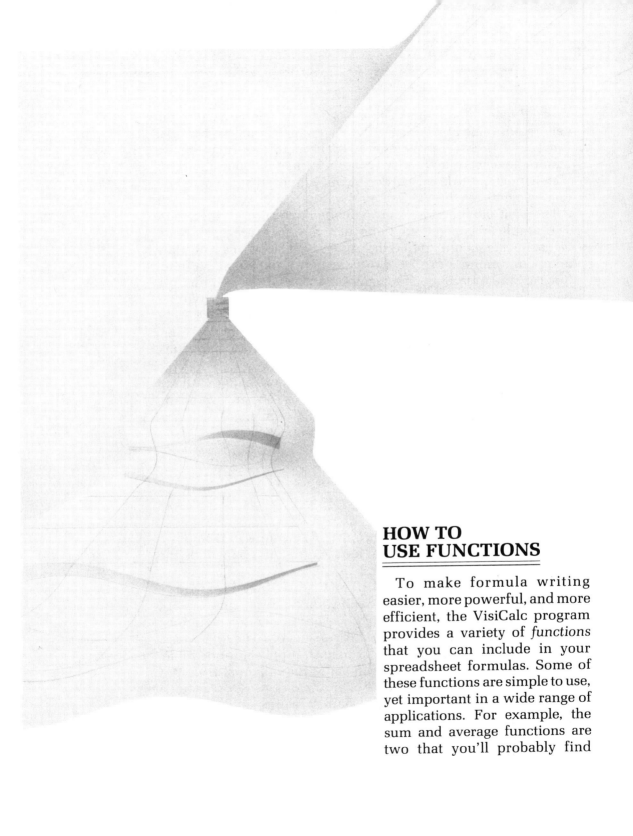

HOW TO
USE FUNCTIONS

To make formula writing easier, more powerful, and more efficient, the VisiCalc program provides a variety of *functions* that you can include in your spreadsheet formulas. Some of these functions are simple to use, yet important in a wide range of applications. For example, the sum and average functions are two that you'll probably find yourself using all the time. Other VisiCalc functions, such as the net present value function, and the trigonometric and exponential functions, are designed for more specialized uses, and may require a more advanced familiarity with mathematics. Your choice of which functions to learn will depend on your particular needs and requirements for the VisiCalc program.

The VisiCalc functions can be divided into several categories. The simple arithmetic functions include sum, average, absolute value, integer, count (to find the number of entries in a list), maximum, and minimum. The more advanced mathematical functions are the square root, the natural and base-10 logarithms, the natural exponent, and the set of trigonometric functions. We will take a careful look at the arithmetic functions in this chapter, and a somewhat more cursory look at the advanced mathematical functions. In Chapters 4 and 5 we will cover other categories of functions.

All of the functions have one thing in common. You have to enter a special "flag" character to alert the VisiCalc program of your intention to use a function. This flag is the "at" symbol on your keyboard (@). You must type this symbol as the first character of any of the functions; for example:

```
@SUM
@AVERAGE
@SIN
@MAX
```

In this context, the @ sign has no intrinsic meaning; it is simply a way of telling VisiCalc that the next word you type will be the name of one of the functions.

In addition, most (but not all) of the VisiCalc functions require that you specify the values that you want the functions to work on. For example, if you're using the average function, you must specify a *list* of values that you want to average. To use the square root function, on the other hand, you need supply only one value. These values are called the *argument* of the function. Different functions require different types of arguments. Most of the functions we'll be examining in this chapter require either a single value, or a list of values as their arguments.

You write the argument of a VisiCalc function within parentheses, directly after the name of the function. The arguments can be expressed in several ways. You might sometimes simply write numbers as the argument of a function. For example:

@SUM(5,7.2,8.34,16)

(Notice that the elements of a *list* are separated by commas.) More often, however, you are likely to use value references as function arguments. For example, you might specify a *range* of positions:

@SUM(B1...B12)

or a *list* of positions:

@SUM(A3,B15,D20)

You can even use *other functions* in the argument of a function:

@SUM(@SQRT(B5),@MIN(A3...A10))

This formula finds the sum of two values: the square root of the value in position B5, and the smallest value in the range of positions from A3 to A10. We will see some realistic examples of using functions as arguments later in this chapter.

Finally, in some cases, an argument will be made of a *combination* of numbers, value references, and other functions. For example, the formula

@SUM(135.22,C3...H3,@MAX(A1...A5))

finds the sum of a list of values; the list consists of a number (135.22), a range of value references (C3...H3), and the maximum value in a range (@MAX(A1...A5)).

In this chapter and the two chapters that follow we will examine many of the VisiCalc functions and see examples of how to use them. In several of the examples, we'll start developing the complete spreadsheets shown back in Chapter 1. You'll recall that these three spreadsheets, which were presented to illustrate the capabilities of the VisiCalc program, all used the same raw data (from Figure 1.1). Now is a good time for you to enter this table of numbers onto a VisiCalc spreadsheet. Since we'll be using these numbers in several different contexts, it would be a good idea to save them in their raw form (that is, without labels or formulas) on a disk file. When you have entered all the numbers, check to make sure you haven't mistyped any. Use the global format command /GF$ to put all the numbers in the dollar-and-cent format.

Make sure you have a data disk in your disk drive. Then type the /SS command to save the spreadsheet. Give the file the name NUMBERS.VC. The spreadsheet will be saved on disk exactly as you see it on the screen.

The first complete example we'll develop is the home application—the one where you've recorded your grocery expenses for the past twelve weeks. Before beginning, you should insert labels for the rows and columns of the table of numbers. Position the cursor at A1, and use the insert command, /IC, to create an empty first column. Then, starting at A1, type the grocery categories:

```
            A
  1 MISC.
  2 CEREALS
  3 MLK/EGGS
  4 CAT FOOD
  5 SUNDRIES
  6 PRODUCE
  7 CIGARETS
  8 MEAT
  9 PASTRIES
 10 LIQUOR
 11 **TOTALS
```

Did you have trouble with the last label—"**TOTALS"? The source of your trouble is this: the asterisk character (*) is normally reserved for formulas (to specify multiplication), and the VisiCalc program doesn't know how to handle it as the first character of a data entry. You need to reassure VisiCalc that you're only entering a label that happens to begin with "*". VisiCalc provides a little trick for entering, as labels, characters that would normally be associated with values. The trick is typing an invisible quotation mark as the first character of the entry. Try it; at A11 type the quotation mark ("). This is what you'll see at the top three lines of the screen:

```
A11
LABEL
□
```

The prompt line shows that VisiCalc is ready to accept a label, but the edit line is blank except for the cue. Now you can type the two asterisks and the word TOTALS.

You can use this same technique any time you want to enter a number (or a symbol like +, −, =, /, @) and have VisiCalc read it as a label.

When you have entered all the labels into column A, then make space at the top of the spreadsheet for the column headings. Go to position A1 and type /IR twice. (This will provide one row for the headings, and one row to keep blank.) You'll want the column headings to be right-justified, so that they'll be easier to identify with the columns of numbers. In position B1, type /FR. The contents line will show that the position is formatted, but otherwise empty:

    B1 /FR

You can now replicate this format over the entire blank row (B2 to M2), so that each heading will be right-justified as soon as you type it in. Type the following sequence of commands:

```
/R                     {invoke replication command}
(return)               {indicate source range: A1...A1}
B1.M1 (return)         {indicate target range: B1...M1}
```

Thoughout the rest of this book you'll see "listings" of VisiCalc commands, in the format illustrated above. On the left are the actual commands that you type into the VisiCalc program. On the right are comments (surrounded by brackets) that will help you understand what the commands are doing. (The comments are, of course, only included in the interest of clarity; they are not actually part of the VisiCalc spreadsheet.) There is nothing *standard* about this format for listing commands. You may choose to follow another format when you start writing down the commands for your own spreadsheets. The only requirements of such a format are that the commands be clear not only to yourself, but also to other people whom you may want to share your listings with.

Enter the column headings, "WEEK #1" to "WEEK#12" in row 1. Finally, go to position A1 and type /TB to fix both the horizontal and the vertical titles. Your spreadsheet should look like Figure 3.1.

We're ready to start trying out the VisiCalc functions on this spreadsheet.

	A	B	C	D	E	F
1		WEEK #1	WEEK #2	WEEK #3	WEEK #4	WEEK #5
2						
3	MISC.	11.18	6.35	8.13	3.56	2.54
4	CEREALS	7.62	7.11	5.59	3.30	0.25
5	MLK/EGGS	11.18	7.62	6.35	4.06	1.02
6	CAT FOOD	1.52	1.78	3.05	4.83	6.86
7	SUNDRIES	4.83	5.33	7.62	9.91	9.91
8	PRODUCE	11.43	11.68	13.97	10.67	10.67
9	CIGARETS	6.60	5.59	7.87	8.89	8.89
10	MEAT	5.59	5.08	5.33	9.30	15.49
11	PASTRIES	6.60	6.35	8.38	7.37	9.55
12	LIQUOR	6.86	7.37	9.40	8.38	8.89
13	**TOTALS					

	G	H	I	J	K	L	M
1	WEEK #6	WEEK #7	WEEK #8	WEEK #9	WEEK#10	WEEK#11	WEEK#12
2							
3	0.76	1.52	2.03	1.78	3.81	7.62	9.40
4	0.00	0.00	0.00	0.51	0.76	5.08	5.59
5	0.25	0.00	0.00	0.51	2.54	5.84	10.16
6	4.83	4.57	3.30	2.79	2.79	2.03	1.02
7	11.18	9.40	7.37	7.37	7.11	6.35	5.08
8	11.94	17.02	13.46	14.22	5.84	9.91	12.95
9	8.38	3.89	7.87	7.11	6.60	7.11	6.10
10	22.86	17.53	17.24	22.10	20.83	6.86	4.06
11	8.89	10.41	12.09	7.87	6.86	7.37	7.62
12	7.62	9.40	10.16	8.38	7.37	9.65	8.89
13							

Figure 3.1: Twelve Weeks of Grocery Expenses

THE ARITHMETIC FUNCTIONS

The grocery expense data are in columns B through M. We're going to create a row of totals at row 13 (i.e., the totals for each week) and a column of totals at column N (i.e., the totals for each grocery category). Then in columns O through R we'll create other columns of statistical data describing your grocery-purchasing behavior. The functions that we'll use to create these columns are summarized in Figure 3.2.

We'll begin by finding the total amount you spent each week. Put the cursor at position B13, which is at the bottom of the column for the first week. Type the function flag, @, and note the

Function	Argument Type	Description
@SUM	list	Finds the sum of the values in the list.
@AVERAGE	list	Finds the average of the values in the list.
@COUNT	list	Finds the number of nonblank values in the list. (Does not count labels.)
@INT	value	Converts the value to an integer (by truncation, not rounding).
@MAX, @MIN	list list	Finds the maximum or minimum values in the list.
@ABS	value	Converts any number (positive or negative) to its positive value (absolute value).

Figure 3.2: The Arithmetic Functions

messages at the top of the screen:

> B13
>
> VALUE
>
> @☐

You can see that the VisiCalc program has read the @ symbol as the beginning of a value. Now type the name of the function, SUM, and the argument, (B3.B12). As usual, you may enter the two addresses either by typing them character-by-character onto the edit line, or by moving the cursor to the actual position that you want to reference in the formula. We want the sum of the values in positions B3 to B12; your edit line should display:

> @SUM(B3...B12)☐

Once you have entered the function, type the return key and look at the result. The total grocery expenditures for week #1 were $73.41.

You can replicate functions in the same way that you replicate any other formula. To illustrate this, type the following sequence (the cursor should be at B13):

/R	{invoke the replication command}
(return)	{indicate the source range: B13...B13}
C13.M13(return)	{indicate the target range: C13...M13}
RR	{both value references are relative}

Notice that the value references in the SUM formula, B3 and B12, must both be replicated as *relative* references.

The row of weekly totals will appear at the bottom of each column. Move the cursor across the entire row to examine the totals:

WEEK #1	WEEK #2	WEEK #3	WEEK #4	WEEK #5	WEEK #6
73.41	64.26	75.69	70.27	74.07	76.71

WEEK #7	WEEK #8	WEEK #9	WEEK #10	WEEK #11	WEEK #12
73.74	73.52	72.64	64.51	67.82	70.87

Notice the contents line as you move the cursor across the row. The value references of the formula change at every entry. For example, at F13, the total for week #5, the contents line displays:

F13(V) @SUM(F3...F12)

We'll now generate a column of totals for the grocery categories. Position the cursor at N1, and type in a column label:

>N1	{position cursor}
/FR	{right-justify format for position}
TOTALS(return)	{enter label}

Next move the cursor down to N3 and enter the summation formula:

>N3	{position cursor}
@SUM(B3.M3)(return)	{enter formula}

The amount 58.68 should appear at N3. You're now ready to replicate this formula over the entire column:

/R	{invoke the replication command}
(return)	{indicate the source range: N3...N3}
N4.N13	{indicate the target range: N4...N13}
RR	{both value references are relative}

Here's what column N should look like now:

	A	N
1		TOTALS
2		
3	MISC.	58.68
4	CEREALS	35.81
5	MLK/EGGS	49.53
6	CAT FOOD	39.37
7	SUNDRIES	91.46
8	PRODUCE	143.76
9	CIGARETS	84.90
10	MEAT	152.27
11	PASTRIES	99.36
12	LIQUOR	102.37
13	**TOTALS	857.51

Notice that position N13 shows a figure for the total amount spent on groceries over the entire period: $857.51.

So far we've learned that functions can be treated like any other kind of formula. Replication is just as easy and perhaps even more powerful, at least in terms of potential results.

To illustrate a few more of the VisiCalc functions, we'll add four more columns of statistics to our grocery spreadsheet. Column O will show the maximum amount spent in any one week for each grocery category; column P will show the minimum. Column Q will be for the average expense in each category; and, finally, column R will show the percent of the 12-week period total ($857.51) represented by each category. All this information may possibly represent a bit more than you've ever really wanted to know about your grocery bill. But one point should be clear by now: VisiCalc's power and versatility lie in the storage and manipulation of numbers; the tasks of deciding what data to produce—and how to use all those numbers in any given application—is up to you, the user.

In creating these additional columns we'll see a new facet of the replication command. Instead of replicating the formulas of each column individually, we'll do them all together in one efficient operation. The first step will be to develop the formulas and enter them onto the spreadsheet for the first grocery category (O3 to R3) and then we will extend the formulas to all the data down the four columns. Place the cursor at O1, and format the four positions O1 to R1 as follows:

>O1	{go to position O1}
/FR	{right-justification format}
/R	{invoke the replication command}
(return)	{indicate the source range: O1...O1}
P1.R1 (return)	{indicate the target range: P1...R1}

Then enter the four headings, "MAX.", "MIN.", "AVE.", and "PERCENT" in the four positions.

The first formula to enter, in position O3, is for the maximum value:

>O3 @MAX(B3.M3)

(The notation >O3 in this case does not imply that you *must* use the GO TO command to position the cursor at O3—although you *may*; rather, it simply means "this is the formula to enter at O3." Also, remember that you must type the return key to enter the formula.)

Position P3 receives the minimum value:

>P3 @MIN(B3.M3)

and, position Q3 the average value:

>Q3 @AVE(B3.M3)

As you enter this last formula, watch the edit line. When you type the left parenthesis character, the VisiCalc program automatically expands the function to its full name:

@AVERAGE(□

In most versions of the VisiCalc program this is a convenience that you can use for entering the name of any function. As soon as you've typed enough letters to identify a function (and distinguish it clearly from any other function), you can just type the parenthesis and VisiCalc will complete the name for you. (Some versions of VisiCalc, however, require that you type the entire function name.)

The first three function entries should now look like this on your spreadsheet:

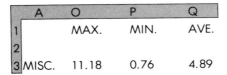

	O	P	Q
	MAX.	MIN.	AVE.
MISC.	11.18	0.76	4.89

The last formula, for the percent of the total expense, will prove to be a bit more complicated. We'll discuss this formula in steps, beginning with the format of the data. The worksheet has a global dollar-and-cent format. Let's say you would prefer to express the percentages with a single, rounded digit after the decimal point. In other words, if a percentage calculates to:

4.59120

you want to express it as:

4.6

The VisiCalc program has no formatting command that will do this for you automatically, but you can write a "rounding" formula using the @INT function. The first time you write a version of this rounding formula you may feel a bit confused. But with practice you'll be able to adapt this formula to any situation.

The rounding process is in four steps:

1. Multiply the number by a factor of 10 so that the decimal point will appear just after the digit that you want to round up or down.

2. Add .5 to the number.

3. Find the integral value of the result (using the @INT function).

4. Divide the number by the same factor of 10 used in step 1.

Here is how this process would work to round the number 4.59120 to the nearest tenth:

1. $4.59120 \times 10 = 45.9120$

2. $45.9120 + .5 = 46.4120$

3. $@INT(46.4120) = 46$

4. $46/10 = 4.6$

You can express all four of these steps in a single VisiCalc formula. Let's say position A1 contains a number that you want to round to the nearest tenth. You would move the cursor to the position that is to receive the rounded value, and type:

@INT(10*A1+.5)/10

This is basically the rounding formula we'll use for our column of percentages, except that we'll have to replace the single value reference (A1, above) with a short formula for calculating the percent. For the first grocery category, this formula will be:

100*N3/N13

because position N13 contains the total expense for the entire period. (Multiplying the fraction by 100 converts it from a decimal to a percentage.) When we combine this formula with the rounding formula, we get:

@INT(1000*N3/N13+.5)/10

Before you type this formula into position R3, you'll have to reformat the position. We want this one column to be formatted differently than the rest of the spreadsheet. In fact, we'd like to return to the *general* numerical format. To do this, position the cursor at R3, and simply type /FG. When we replicate the formula at column R, the format will also be applied down the column.

Now type the formula, and look at the result. The "miscellaneous" grocery category represents 6.8% of the total expenditures for the twelve-week period.

We're now ready to replicate our four formulas down their corresponding columns to complete our work on this spreadsheet. Position the cursor at O3 and type /R. The prompt line shows:

REPLICATE: SOURCE RANGE OR RETURN

Up to now we've always typed the return key at this point to tell the VisiCalc program that we had only one formula to replicate. This time we have the four formulas, and so the replication process will be somewhat different. Type:

.R3 (return)

to specify the source range. The edit line should now look like this:

O3...R3: ☐

For the target range, type:

O4.O13 (return)

Now, in the third phase of the replication command, the VisiCalc program will guide you through the four source formulas one by one so that you can specify how the value references should be treated in each formula. For each of the first three formulas, you'll type:

RR

because the @MAX, @MIN, and @AVERAGE functions all have variable (i.e., relative) ranges. The last formula however, will require:

RN

The N ("no change") indicates that the value reference N13—the total expenses for the period—is a constant in this formula.

You may want to add a title and some underlining to improve the clarity and presentation of your spreadsheet. (Use the /IR command to insert rows at the top of the spreadsheet.) The columns that we have created in this chapter are shown in Figure 3.3. Compare this figure with the data on your spreadsheet to make sure nothing has gone wrong in your formulas.

	A	N	O	P	Q	R
1			WEEKLY GROCERY EXPENSES			
2			30 MAY TO 21 AUGUST			
3		===				
4		TOTALS	MAX.	MIN.	AVE.	PERCENT
5		======	====	====	====	=======
6	MISC.	58.68	11.18	0.76	4.89	6.8
7	CEREALS	35.81	7.62	0.00	2.98	4.2
8	MLK/EGGS	49.53	11.18	0.00	4.13	5.8
9	CAT FOOD	39.37	6.86	1.02	3.28	4.6
10	SUNDRIES	91.46	11.18	4.83	7.62	10.7
11	PRODUCE	143.76	17.02	5.84	11.98	16.8
12	CIGARETS	84.90	8.89	3.89	7.08	9.9
13	MEAT	152.27	22.86	4.06	12.69	17.8
14	PASTRIES	99.36	12.09	6.35	8.28	11.6
15	LIQUOR	102.37	10.16	6.86	8.53	11.9
16	**TOTALS	857.51	76.71	64.26	71.46	100

Figure 3.3: The Formula Columns from the Grocery Spreadsheet

THE ADVANCED
MATHEMATICAL FUNCTIONS

The mathematical functions that we'll discuss in this section extend the usefulness of the VisiCalc program to applications in science, engineering, and statistics. Even if you never intend to use these functions, you should not skip reading this presentation, because we will cover a few points that are of general interest.

The trigonometric and exponential functions are described briefly in Figure 3.4. As an exercise to illustrate a couple of these functions in action, in a somewhat complex formula, we will develop a spreadsheet of the "normal distribution" curve. You have probably come in contact at one point or another with the so-called "bell-shaped curve" that is used to describe normal statistical distribution. We will write a VisiCalc formula for the equation of this curve, and then use the /F∗ command to create a graphic representation.

The normal distribution formula contains a natural exponential

Function	Argument Type	Description
@EXP	value	Raises e to the power of the value argument. (Type @EXP(1) to see VisiCalc's value of e.)
@LN	value	Finds the natural exponent (base e).
@LOG10	value	Finds the base-10 logarithm.
@SQRT	value	Finds the square root of the value.
@SIN, @COS, @TAN	value (in radians)	Trigonometric Sine, Cosine, and Tangent functions. (To convert degrees to radians, use: degrees ∗ (@PI / 180).)
@ATAN, @ACOS, @ASIN	value	Trigonometric Arctangent, Arccosine, and Arcsine. (All three functions return values in radians.)
@PI	no argument	Supplies the value of pi.

Figure 3.4: Advanced Mathematical Functions

in the numerator and the square root of pi in the denominator.[1] Never mind if you don't know exactly what this means; the main point of this illustration is to show how a complicated equation can be calculated—and graphed—using the VisiCalc program. The formula we'll use on the VisiCalc spreadsheet is:

@EXP(− (A1^2)/2)/@SQRT(2 * @PI)

Notice that this formula contains three functions—the natural exponential, @EXP; the square root, @SQRT; and the function that simply supplies the value of pi, @PI. The @PI function is one of several VisiCalc functions that require no argument.

To prepare for the normal distribution spreadsheet, make sure you have saved any current information that you don't want to lose (/SS), and then type /CY to clear the screen. We are going to look at the distribution formula over a range of −2 to +2, in increments of .2. Type the value −2 into position A1. In A2 type the formula:

+A1 + .2

Then replicate this formula over the positions A3 to A21:

/R	{invoke replication command}
(return)	{indicate source range: A2...A2}
A3.A21 (return)	{indicate target range: A3...A21}
R	{the value reference is relative}

Now move the cursor to position B1 and type the normal distribution formula:

@EXP(− (A1^2)/2)/@SQRT(2 * @PI)

Make sure you type all the parentheses in the right places; this is an example of a formula that would be very different with misplaced or missing parentheses. (Do you see why?) Then replicate the formula down the B column, from B2 to B21:

/R	{invoke the replication command}
(return)	{indicate source range: B1...B1}
B2.B21 (return)	{indicate target range: B2...B21}
R	{the value reference is relative}

---

[1] $$y = \frac{e^{\frac{-x^2}{2}}}{\sqrt{2\pi}}$$

This replication may take your computer a while to perform, because the formula is complicated.

Now split the window at column C and increase the column width of the window on the right to 20 spaces:

>C1   {place cursor at C1}

/WV   {split the window vertically}

;   {toggle the cursor into the right-hand window}

/GC20   {increase column width to 20}

Now we're ready to create the graph. You may remember how simple it was to display the graph in Chapter 2. We simply reformatted a column of numbers (/GF∗) in the right-hand window. The reason that was possible was that the numbers in the column were in a convenient range—between 1 and 12. If you look at column B of our current spreadsheet, you'll see that we're clearly dealing with a more difficult situation here. The numbers range from about .05 to .4. If we simply reformatted them with the /GF∗ command, we would get no graph at all, because the numbers are too small. For this reason, we have to set up a scale factor to increase all the numbers proportionally; they will still represent the same equation, but VisiCalc will be able to make a graph out of them.

The scale factor is based on deciding how many asterisks will represent the *largest* number in the range of numbers. Let's arbitrarily choose 15. So, the largest number in column B will be displayed as a row of 15 asterisks. The other values will be displayed as 15 or fewer asterisks.

We'll use the @MAX function to find the largest number in the range B1 to B21. Thus, if we multiply each number by:

15/@MAX(B1...B21)

then we will have a new set of numbers that range in value from 0 to 15. The basic formula we would enter at C1, then, is:

(15/@MAX(B1...B21))∗B1

But there is one added complication. The /F∗ command truncates numbers, rather than rounding them, when it converts integers to a row of asterisks. This decreases the accuracy of a curve. So, we should use the @INT function to include rounding in our formula:

@INT((15/@MAX(B1...B21))∗B1+.5)

This, finally, is the equation that you should type into position C1.

Then type /F✶ to convert the result into graphics format. Now you can replicate the formula to create the bell-shaped curve:

/R	{invoke the replication command}
(return)	{indicate source range: C1...C1}
C2.C21	{indicate target range: C2...C21}
NNR	{the range of @MAX is constant; the value reference B1 is relative}

The result of this replication is shown in Figure 3.5.

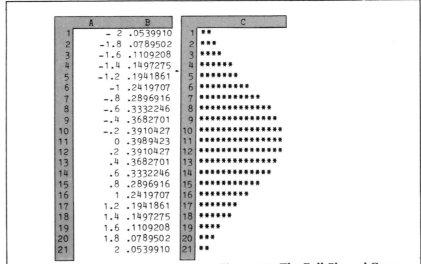

Figure 3.5: The Bell-Shaped Curve

SUMMARY

The VisiCalc program is enriched with a set of functions that you can incorporate into formulas to perform many arithmetic tasks more efficiently. Most of the functions require arguments of a range, a list, or a value. These arguments may be expressed as numbers, value references, or as other functions.

The most commonly used functions are the simplest ones, such as @SUM and @AVERAGE. The VisiCalc program also includes other functions, though, for more specialized use.

In Chapter 4 we will investigate two other categories of functions—the *search* functions, @LOOKUP and @CHOOSE, and the *logical* functions.

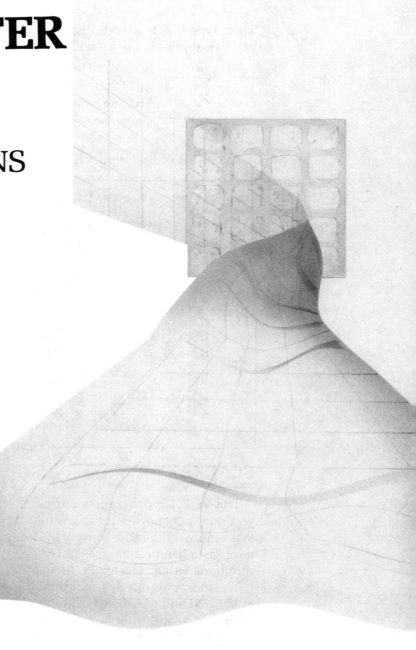

CHAPTER FOUR

VISICALC
FUNCTIONS
(PART II)

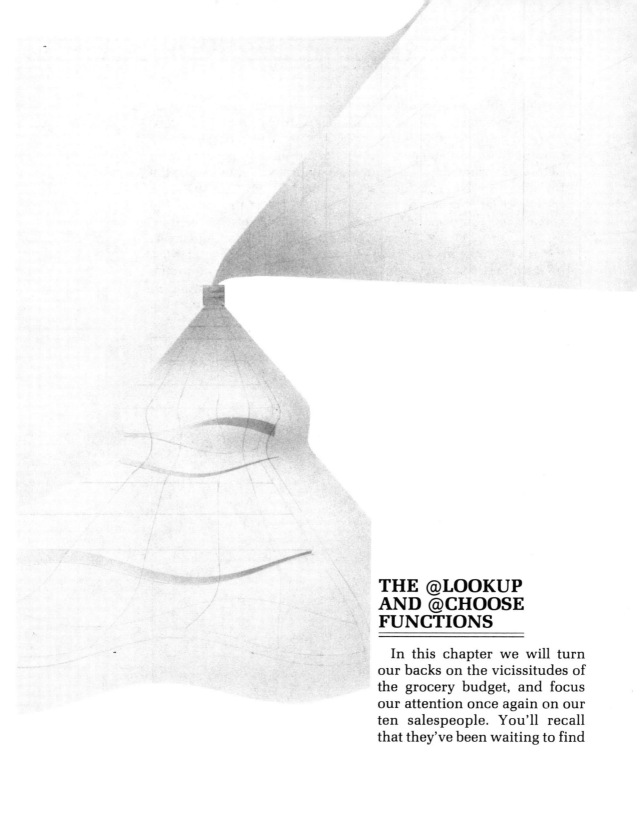

THE @LOOKUP
AND @CHOOSE
FUNCTIONS

In this chapter we will turn our backs on the vicissitudes of the grocery budget, and focus our attention once again on our ten salespeople. You'll recall that they've been waiting to find out which of them, due to less than vigorous annual sales records, will have to start pounding the sidewalk in search of a new job.

We're going to be building a spreadsheet based on all twelve months of sales data, so rather than use the spreadsheet from Chapter 2 (which described only one month) you should load the raw data—stored in the file that you named NUMBERS.VC—into your VisiCalc spreadsheet. Insert a column at the left of the spreadsheet for the names of the salespeople (Baker, Smith, Flint, Brown, Vern, Marlow, Harper, Fleming, Nash, White), and insert five rows at the top to make room for column headings and titles. In positions B4 to M4, type in the three-letter abbreviations for the names of the months, in a right-justified format. At position A4 type /TB to fix the titles in both directions. Figure 4.1 shows the starting-point of your spreadsheet.

	A	B	C	D	E	F
4		JAN	FEB	MAR	APR	MAY
5		===	===	===	===	===
6	BAKER	11.18	6.35	8.13	3.56	2.54
7	SMITH	7.62	7.11	5.59	3.30	0.25
8	FLINT	11.18	7.62	6.35	4.06	1.02
9	BROWN	1.52	1.78	3.05	4.83	6.86
10	VERN	4.83	5.33	7.62	9.91	9.91
11	MARLOW	11.43	11.68	13.97	10.67	10.67
12	HARPER	6.60	5.59	7.87	8.89	8.89
13	FLEMING	5.59	5.08	5.33	9.30	15.49
14	NASH	6.60	6.35	8.38	7.37	9.55
15	WHITE	6.86	7.37	9.40	8.38	8.89

	G	H	I	J	K	L	M
4	JUN	JUL	AUG	SEP	OCT	NOV	DEC
5	===	===	===	===	===	===	===
6	0.76	1.52	2.03	1.78	3.81	7.62	9.40
7	0.00	0.00	0.00	0.51	0.76	5.08	5.59
8	0.25	0.00	0.00	0.51	2.54	5.84	10.16
9	4.83	4.57	3.30	2.79	2.79	2.03	1.02
10	11.18	9.40	7.37	7.37	7.11	6.35	5.08
11	11.94	17.02	13.46	14.22	5.84	9.91	12.95
12	8.38	3.89	7.87	7.11	6.60	7.11	6.10
13	22.86	17.53	17.24	22.10	20.83	6.86	4.06
14	8.89	10.41	12.09	7.87	6.86	7.37	7.62
15	7.62	9.40	10.16	8.38	7.37	9.65	8.89

Figure 4.1: The Sales Spreadsheet with Twelve Months of Data

Our first concern will be to calculate the total annual salary, including bonus, for each salesperson. To do so, we must learn how to use yet another VisiCalc function—@LOOKUP. The @LOOKUP function, unlike any other function we've seen so far, requires two different types of arguments—a value, and a range. The function appears in the following form:

@LOOKUP(value, range)

The @LOOKUP function was almost certainly inspired by that insidious document that we all have to study at least once a year—the tax table. The format is familiar; there's a column of income figures on the left, and a column of tax amounts on the right. You use the table by looking down the income column until you find the two entries that delimit your own income. Then you slide your finger over to the column on the right to find out how much money you owe in taxes.

The @LOOKUP function performs precisely this same searching task, except that its operation is not, of course, limited to tax tables. To use the @LOOKUP function, you have to set up a pair of columns (or rows) of corresponding data someplace on your spreadsheet. This is where the bonus table—which we first saw in Chapter 1—comes in.

Let's say we enter the bonus table onto our worksheet in columns M and N, in the rows beneath the sales data:

	M	N
21	BONUS TABLE	
22	- - - - - - - - - - - -	
23	0.00	0.25
24	50.00	1.00
25	75.00	1.50
26	100.00	2.25
27	125.00	3.00
28	150.00	3.50

The table works in the following way: if one of the salespeople has annual sales of, say, $85,000 then we look down column M until $85,000 (or 85, since the numbers are in units of $1000) falls between two of the entries. When we find that spot, we then look across in column N, at the row corresponding to the *lesser* of the two delimiting entries in column M, and find the bonus. For annual sales of $85,000, the bonus is $1,500 (since 85 falls between 75 and 100).

To find this value using the @LOOKUP function, we write:

@LOOKUP(85, M23...M28)

The first argument, 85, is the value that we are searching for. The second argument, M23...M28, is the range of values that we need to search through. If the range is a column, as it is in this example, then @LOOKUP returns the corresponding value from the column at the immediate *right*, as shown on the bonus lookup table. (If the range is a row, then the value comes from the row directly *below*.)

Before we can use the bonus table, we need a column of total sales for each salesperson. These values are the ones that we will search for in the lookup table. We'll put this information in column N:

>N4 /FR TOTALS	{heading at position N4}
>N5 /FR "======	{underline heading}
>N6 @SUM(B6.M6)	{enter summation formula at N6}
/R	{invoke replication command}
(return)	{source range: N6...N6}
N7.N15 (return)	{target range: N7...N15}
RR	{B6 and M6 are both relative}

Now, if you haven't already entered the bonus table you should do so, beginning at position M21. We're ready to use the @LOOKUP function to display the bonuses in column O. Start by entering a heading:

>O4 /FR BONUS	{heading at position O4}
>O5 /FR "=====	{underline heading}

The lookup formula, in position O6, will look like this:

@LOOKUP(N6, M23...M28)

This instructs the VisiCalc program to take the total sales entry at N6, find its location in the range of values at M23 to M28 on the bonus lookup table, and return the corresponding bonus value from the entries at N23 to N28. (In other words, VisiCalc searches through the specified values in column M, and then returns a value from the column at the immediate right, column N.) When you enter the formula, the resulting value displayed at O6 should be 1.00. For total annual sales of $58,680, salesperson Baker gets a bonus of $1,000.

Now we can replicate the lookup formula to find the bonuses for all the salespeople. The only tricky part of the replication is the third phase, where we have to specify which value references are relative and which are constant. Clearly N6, the total sales figure, is relative—we want to use a different amount for each salesperson's bonus. But the value references of the range, M23...M28, are constant. We use the same bonus table for everyone. Here are the replication instructions (make sure the cursor is at O6):

/R	{invoke the replication command}
(return)	{source range: O6...O6}
O7.O15 (return)	{target range: O7...O15}
RNN	{N6 is relative; M23 and M28 do not change}

To complete the spreadsheet we should add a column of total salaries. The base annual salary is $12,000, and the commission is 5%. We'll store this information just above the bonus table, in positions N18 and N19, respectively:

	M	N
17	=================	
18	BASE	12.00
19	COMM.	0.05
20	=================	

The formula for the total salary is:

bonus + base + (commission rate × total sales)

We'll enter the VisiCalc equivalent of this formula into position P6:

+O6 + N18 + (N19 ∗ N6)

and then replicate the formula for all the salespeople:

/R	{invoke replication command}
(return)	{source range: P6...P6}
P7.P15 (return)	{target range: P7...P15}
RNNR	{O6 and N6 are relative; N18 and N19 do not change}

Finally, we can add a title at the top of the spreadsheet in the rows we reserved for that purpose when we first began. The salary columns of the spreadsheet are shown in Figure 4.2. We'll be continuing to build on this spreadsheet, so make sure you save it on disk before clearing the screen.

The VisiCalc program supplies another function that is designed for searching—the @CHOOSE function. Like the @LOOKUP function, @CHOOSE requires two arguments, in the following form:

@CHOOSE(value, list)

Notice that @CHOOSE searches through a *list,* rather than a *range.* A list, you will recall, is not restricted to a contiguous row or column of values, but rather can include diverse sources of data. @CHOOSE uses its value argument as an ordinal pointer into its list argument, and returns the indicated value in the list. For example, in the following formula:

@CHOOSE(5, N7,P13,S1...S7)

@CHOOSE would return the 5th element in the list argument expressed as N7, P13, S1...S7. (Can you see what element the 5th would be?)

	A	M	N	O	P
1			ANNUAL SALES SALARIES		
2			JAN TO DEC		
3	=================================				
4		DEC	TOTALS	BONUS	TOT SAL
5		===	======	=====	=======
6	BAKER	9.40	58.68	1.00	15.93
7	SMITH	5.59	35.81	0.25	14.04
8	FLINT	10.16	49.53	0.25	14.73
9	BROWN	1.02	39.37	0.25	14.22
10	VERN	5.08	91.46	1.50	18.07
11	MARLOW	12.95	143.76	3.00	22.19
12	HARPER	6.10	84.90	1.50	17.75
13	FLEMING	4.06	152.27	3.50	23.11
14	NASH	7.62	99.36	1.50	18.47
15	WHITE	8.89	102.37	2.25	19.37
16					
17		=================			
18		BASE	12.00		
19		COMM.	0.05		
20		=================			
21		BONUS TABLE			
22		-----------------			
23		0.00	0.25		
24		50.00	1.00		
25		75.00	1.50		
26		100.00	2.25		
27		125.00	3.00		
28		150.00	3.50		

Figure 4.2: Annual Salaries for Salespeople

The @LOOKUP and @CHOOSE functions are clearly indispensable in applications where a single value must be found and returned from a table or list of values. We will see additional uses for @LOOKUP later in this chapter.

THE LOGICAL FUNCTIONS

The VisiCalc logical functions are in a separate category of their own. They may seem a little intimidating at first glance, but they are actually quite easy to learn to use, and can add significantly to your power of control over the numbers you enter into your VisiCalc spreadsheet.

The main commodity of the logical functions is not numerical values, but rather *logical values*, which are either *true* or *false*. Logical statements in VisiCalc are used to compare two values. The "verbs" of the logical statements—that is, the symbols that indicate how you are comparing the two values—are the following:

$$=\quad \{equals\}$$
$$<\quad \{is\ less\ than\}$$
$$>\quad \{is\ greater\ than\}$$
$$<=\quad \{is\ less\ than\ or\ equal\ to\}$$
$$>=\quad \{is\ greater\ than\ or\ equal\ to\}$$
$$<>\quad \{is\ not\ equal\ to\}$$

These symbols are sometimes called the *logical operators*. Here are several examples of statements that use these operators:

$$B1 = 5$$
$$C7 <= M3$$
$$A1 <> A2$$
$$G11 > 10$$

Each of these statements is either true or false. Statements like these can be written directly into VisiCalc logical functions; they result in logical values of true or false.

The major logical functions are summarized in Figure 4.3. The @IF function is probably the most important of all of them, and the one that you'll find yourself using the most often. It is similar in structure to IF statements in programming languages, such as BASIC or Pascal. Such statements in these languages provide two alternative paths of action; the choice of paths depends on the evaluation (to TRUE or FALSE) of a logical statement:

IF (logical statement) THEN (action#1) ELSE (action#2)

If the logical statement is true, then action #1 is performed; if the logical statement is false, then action #2 is performed.

The VisiCalc @IF function takes the following form:

@IF(logical value, value, value)

It places one of two different values in a spreadsheet position, depending on the logical value. For example, let's say you've

Function	Arguments	Description
@IF	(logical value),value,value	If the logical value is true, the function returns the first value argument; if false, the second.
@AND	list of logical values	If *all* the logical values in the argument are true, the function returns a true value; otherwise, a false value.
@OR	list of logical values	If *any one or more* of the logical values in the argument are true, the function returns a true value; if *all* the logical values are false, then the function returns a false value.
@NOT	logical value	Returns a false value if the logical value in the argument is true; returns a true value if the logical value is false.
@TRUE	no argument	Returns a true value; can be used either as an argument in a logical function, or as a value entry to display TRUE on the spreadsheet.
@FALSE	no argument	Returns a false value; can be used either as an argument in a logical function, or as a value entry to display FALSE on the spreadsheet.

Figure 4.3: The Logical Functions

typed the fcllowing formula into position B2:

@IF(B1>1000,25,10)

You can read this statement as follows: "If the value at position B1 is greater than 1000, then put the value 25 in position B2; otherwise (if B1 is less than or equal to 1000) put the value 10 in B2." In other words, if the current value of B1 is something over 1000, say 1500, this is what you'll see on your spreadsheet:

	B
1	1500
2	25

But if B1 is less than (or equal to) 1000, say 750, you'll see:

	B
1	750
2	10

Sometimes you'll want to make the action of an @IF function depend on a more complicated logical statement. You may want to combine two (or more) equalities or inequalities to decide which value to return from the @IF function. In such a case, you can use the @AND or @OR function as part of the argument of the @IF function.

Consider a quick example. Let's say you are trying to decide where to go for your summer vacation this year, and you have listed several criteria (climate, cost, recreational facilities, and so on) that you intend to base your decision on. You're awarding points to each of half-a-dozen potential vacation spots, based on how well they match with your criteria. You're tabulating this scoring system on a VisiCalc spreadsheet. When all the scores are determined, you'll study them, perhaps add a subjective fudge factor here or there (which only you, not your computer, can supply), and then make your choice.

For the climate criterion, you have entered what you consider to be the ideal average temperature range—78° to 95°—in positions A19 and A20:

	A
18	TEMP.
19	78
20	95

You are awarding 10 points to any city that falls within that range. In column B of your spreadsheet, you're recording the average temperature of each city, and the resulting points scored in column C.

At position C1 you type the following formula:

@IF(@AND(B1>=A19,B1<=A20),10,0)

The AND function is a logical statement that returns a true or a false value. @AND returns a true if *all* of the statements in its argument are true. If *any* of the statements in the argument are false (even one!), @AND returns a false value. So, we can read this VisiCalc formula as follows: "If the value at B1 is greater than or equal to the value at A19, *and* less than or equal to the value at A20, put the value 10 in position C1; otherwise put the value 0 in position C1." In other words, if the temperature recorded at B1 is within the ideal range of temperatures shown in A19 and A20, the vacation spot gets 10 points; otherwise it gets no points.

We can test this formula by putting different values in position B1. Start with 88, a temperature within the desired range. Here's what you'll see:

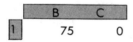

The points are awarded, as they should be. Now try 75:

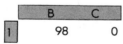

Too cold; no points. Finally, try 98:

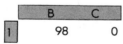

Too hot; no points. So, the @IF function combined with @AND works just as we expected it to.

The @OR function returns a value of true if *any one or more* of the logical values in its argument is true. It turns out that we could have produced exactly the same results in awarding points for the temperature criterion if we had written our formula using the @OR function, rather than @AND:

@IF(@OR(B1<A19,B1>A20),0,10)

In this case, @OR returns a true value if the temperature value at

B1 is *outside* of the desired temperature range. Notice that the two value arguments of the @IF function have been reversed: a true means no points; a false, 10 points.

We will now return, for the last time, to our salesperson spreadsheet and look at a second example of the @IF function. The situation we'll assume is this: You need to set up some kind of objective criterion for determining which salespeople are not doing well. Of course, you will probably combine this criterion with more subjective judgments before you decide on any action to take. But the objective criterion, at least, can be worked out on the VisiCalc spreadsheet.

The criterion will be based on three averages that you will calculate from the spreadsheet sales data:

1. the average total annual sales per salesperson,

2. the average of all the best-single-month sales figures for each salesperson (i.e., find the best monthly sales figure out of the twelve months for each salesperson, and average all these figures for the ten salespeople), and

3. the average of the worst-single-month sales figures for each salesperson.

Any salesperson whose record does not match or exceed the average in at least one of these categories will be placed on probation and under review.

The first of the three averages can be calculated directly from the column of total annual sales figures—column N—which we included in the spreadsheet earlier in this chapter. We'll place this figure in position R18. Here is the formula:

   @AVERAGE(N6...N15)

You might also want to identify this value with a label in position Q18:

Q	R
18 AVE.TOT=	85.75

To calculate the other two averages, we'll have to set up columns for the best and worst single-month sales records for each salesperson. We'll use the @MAX and @MIN functions to produce these columns. The best-single-month figures will go in column

Q, and the worst in column R. Here is the sequence of instructions for these two columns:

```
>Q4 /FR BEST          {right-justified column heading}
>Q5 /FR "====         {underline heading}
>Q6 @MAX(B6.M6)       {maximum value formula}
>R4 /FR WORST         {right-justified column heading}
>R5 /FR "=====        {underline heading}
>R6 @MIN(B6.M6)       {minimum value formula}
>Q6 /R                {invoke replication command}
.R6 (return)          {source range: Q6...R6}
Q7.Q15 (return)       {target range: Q7...Q15}
RR RR                 {B6 and M6 relative in both formulas}
```

Notice that we have replicated both of the formulas at once.

Next, we'll put the averages of the "best" and "worst" columns in positions Q17 and R17, respectively. The formulas are:

```
>Q17 @AVERAGE(Q6...Q15)
>R17 @AVERAGE(R7...R15)
```

To identify these two values, you may want to go to position A17 and insert a label such as "∗∗AVE." The averages should look like this:

	A	Q	R
4		BEST	WORST
5		====	=====
.	.	.	.
.	.	.	.
.	.	.	.
16			
17	∗∗AVE.	11.90	3.36
18		AVE.TOT=	85.75

So you've now calculated the three averages on which you're going to base the salesperson evaluation formula. Position the cursor at S4, and type the column heading "< AVE." ("less than average") and underline it in position S5. The formula itself will go into position S6. What is the best way to indicate which salespeople have below-average records? One good way is simply to place a "flag" of some sort in the rows containing those records. We have seen that /F∗ is a convenient format command that changes numbers to asterisks; perhaps we could use /F* to produce the flags.

Place the cursor at position S6, and type /F*. We can write our @IF formula using either @AND or @OR, but in this case @AND seems more straightforward. We'll write the formula for the first salesperson, Baker, and then replicate it down the column for the rest of the salespeople.

Three conditions must be true for a salesperson to be put on probation; the total annual sales for that person must be less than the average annual sales:

N6 < R18

the best-month sales for that person must be less than the average best-month sales:

Q6 < Q17

and, the worst-month sales for that person must be less than the average worst-month sales:

R6 < R17

We'll combine these three conditions in one @AND function:

@AND(N6<R18,Q6<Q17,R6<R17)

If this @AND function returns a true value for any given salesperson, then the sales record is below average in all three categories, and we want to flag it. Here's how we'll produce the flag. We'll write the @IF function so that a 2 will be put in the position for a true value, and a 0 for a false value. Under the /F* format, the 2 will become a double asterisk, and the 0 will remain blank. Here, then, is the formula to type into position S6:

@IF(@AND(N6<R18,Q6<Q17,R6<R17),2,0)

This @IF function contains the three required arguments: the logical value comes from the @AND function; the value corresponding to *true* is 2; the value corresponding to *false* is 0. A double asterisk should appear in position S6 on the spreadsheet, indicating that Baker's sales record is below average.

Finally, we will replicate this formula to apply it to all the salespeople. The target range is S7 to S15. In the third phase of the replication, you'll have to think carefully about the value references; three of them are relative (the individual sales records) and three of them remain constant for the entire replication (the averages):

RNRNRN

The results are shown in Figure 4.4. Notice the title that has been added in row 1, above the three columns of information we have created in this section. Since a long spreadsheet is scrolled onto the VisiCalc screen in bits and pieces, it is perfectly all right to include several different titles, describing each part of the spreadsheet.

```
            A       Q       R       S
  1             SALESPEOPLE EVALUATIONS
  2
  3       ===================================
  4               BEST   WORST < AVE.
  5               ====   ===== ======
  6  BAKER       11.18    0.76 **
  7  SMITH        7.62    0.00 **
  8  FLINT       11.18    0.00 **
  9  BROWN        6.86    1.02 **
 10  VERN        11.18    4.83
 11  MARLOW      17.02    5.84
 12  HARPER       8.89    3.89
 13  FLEMING     22.86    4.06
 14  NASH        12.09    6.35
 15  WHITE       10.16    6.86
 16
 17  **AVE.      11.90    3.36
 18          AVE.TOT=    85.75
```

Figure 4.4: The Salesperson Evaluation

GETTING ALONG WITHOUT THE LOGICAL FUNCTIONS

Some versions of the VisiCalc program do not include the logical functions. If you have one of these versions, then you'll have to be a bit more creative in situations that call for the kinds of comparisons and operations that the logical functions perform.

Whether or not your VisiCalc program supplies the logical functions, you should always try to think of VisiCalc in the larger context of your personal computer. Sometimes you will encounter applications which, while *possible* to solve using VisiCalc, would be infinitely easier to perform in a high-level programming language, such as BASIC or Pascal. True, there are VisiCalc virtuosos around who would have you believe that VisiCalc is the final answer to all your programming needs. But this philosophy may in fact be a disservice to the VisiCalc program. We have seen in many examples that the elegance of VisiCalc lies in its simplicity; but this only remains true for the kinds of applications that VisiCalc was designed to handle.

In general, a language like BASIC is much better suited than the VisiCalc program to performing tasks that require complicated logic and multiple paths of decisions. If you have such a task, you should consider using VisiCalc for the data input, creating a DIF file to store the data on disk, and then writing a BASIC program to process the data. It is fairly easy to write general-purpose BASIC programs to read and write DIF files (as we will be seeing in Chapters 6, 7, and 8). Once these programs are available to you, you may find that the VisiCalc program and BASIC are ideal partners for many of your data processing needs.

But what if you are working out an application that calls for some simple logical decisions—within the realm of the VisiCalc program—and your version of VisiCalc does not have the logical functions? Often, with a little thought, you'll come up with adequate solutions that use other VisiCalc functions. Let's look at a few examples.

The @MAX and @MIN functions can take the place of some @IF inequalities. In fact, in some cases, using @MAX or @MIN is much more direct. For example, the following two formulas produce the same results:

@IF((A1<100),A1,100)

@MIN(A1,100)

In both cases, if the value at position A1 is less than 100, then the function returns A1; otherwise the function returns 100.

In slightly more complicated situations, we can use @LOOKUP to simulate @IF. The following @IF statement is a case in point:

@IF(A1<100,10,25)

This statement returns 10 if the value at A1 is smaller than 100, or 25 if A1 is greater than or equal to 100. We can set up a lookup table that contains the values 10 and 25 in the right-hand column:

	C	D
1	0	10
2	100	25

Then, the following formula uses this lookup table to produce the same results as the @IF statement above:

@LOOKUP(A1,C1...C2)

You can see what will happen for different values of A1: As long as A1 is smaller than 100 then @LOOKUP returns the value at position D1, i.e., 10. For values of A1 that are greater than or equal to 100, @LOOKUP returns the value at D2, i.e., 25. Type this formula onto a practice spreadsheet, into position E1, and try it out on different values of A1. If you experiment long enough, you might discover a problem. The @LOOKUP version only works if A1 is greater than or equal to zero. If you type a value less than zero into position A1, then the @LOOKUP function returns a message—NA, meaning Not Available—rather than a value in position E1. This is because the range of your lookup table does not include negative numbers. To remedy this situation, you could simply revise the lookup table; specifically, C1 would have to contain a negative number large enough to cover any expected situation.

Continue experimenting with this formula by replacing the current value at C1 with the value −9999999. Now try putting some small negative numbers in position A1. The @LOOKUP formula will now correctly simulate the @IF formula, by returning a value of 10.

We can also use the @LOOKUP function, in combination with the absolute value function, @ABS, as a substitute for *equalities* in @IF statements. Let's say we want to test whether two values—in positions A1 and A2—are equal. If they are, we want to place a 1 in position B1; if not, a 0. The @IF statement that would do this is:

@IF(A1=A2,1,0)

To produce the same results without @IF, we can subtract one value from the other. If their difference is zero, then we know they are equal. If they are not equal, however, the subtraction could produce either a positive or a negative result, depending on which number is the larger. In order to use the result of the subtraction with the @LOOKUP function, we would like some way of making sure the difference will always be negative. To do so, we use the absolute value function.

You'll recall that the @ABS function returns the positive value of any number. Knowing this, you can see that the following expression will always be negative, except when A1 equals A2:

$$-@ABS(A1-A2)$$

We can create a lookup table that will return a value of 0 for negative numbers, and a value of 1 for zero:

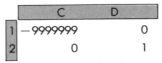

As with the previous lookup table, we have to be careful that the negative value at C1 is sufficiently large to cover any likely situation. Now we can write our formula:

$$@LOOKUP(-@ABS(A1-A2),C1...C2)$$

Type this formula onto your spreadsheet at position E1 and test it with some values at A1 and A2. Because of the @ABS function, it doesn't matter which of the two values is the larger. This function will test for the equality of any two numbers, including negative numbers and zero.

Another substitute has been suggested for testing equalities[1]; this method is perhaps more convenient (it doesn't require the lookup table), but it is less reliable than the @LOOKUP and @ABS method. Here is the formula:

$$@INT(A1/A2)*@INT(A2/A1)$$

This formula is based on the fact that the integral value of a fraction between 0 and 1 is 0. Thus, if A1 is not equal to A2, then one of the two @INT expressions will result in a value of 0. On the other hand, if A1 equals A2, the formula will result in a value of 1. This method has two limitations, one obvious and one not so obvious:

1. A value of 0 in either position A1 or A2 results in an error condition—the VisiCalc program will display the message ERROR on the spreadsheet. (0 in the denominator of a fraction is illegal.)

2. If A1 equals $-$A2, the formula will result in a value of 1, for equality. For example, if A1 contains 7 and A2 contains -7, the formula will result in 1.

---

[1] SATN, Vol.1, No.4, March/April 1982, p.6.

You will undoubtedly think of—or read about—many more methods of simulating the logical functions. Some of the methods will be of general usefulness, available to many different applications. Others will be designed to solve one specific problem. With a little ingenuity, most simple decisions involving logical statements can be worked out with or without the aid of the VisiCalc logical functions.

SUMMARY

The search functions—@LOOKUP and @CHOOSE—are convenient for finding a single value in a table or in a list of values. The logical functions, on the other hand, evaluate logical statements and then choose between two values. A number of clever substitutes can be devised for those versions of the VisiCalc program that do not contain the logical functions.

In using all of these functions, you should be careful to stay within the turf of the VisiCalc program. It is often tempting to try to perform a task in VisiCalc that could be easier to accomplish using some other programming tool.

In Chapter 5 we will discuss some general concepts about planning VisiCalc spreadsheets, and we will introduce several other VisiCalc functions.

CHAPTER FIVE

PLANNING VISICALC SPREADSHEETS

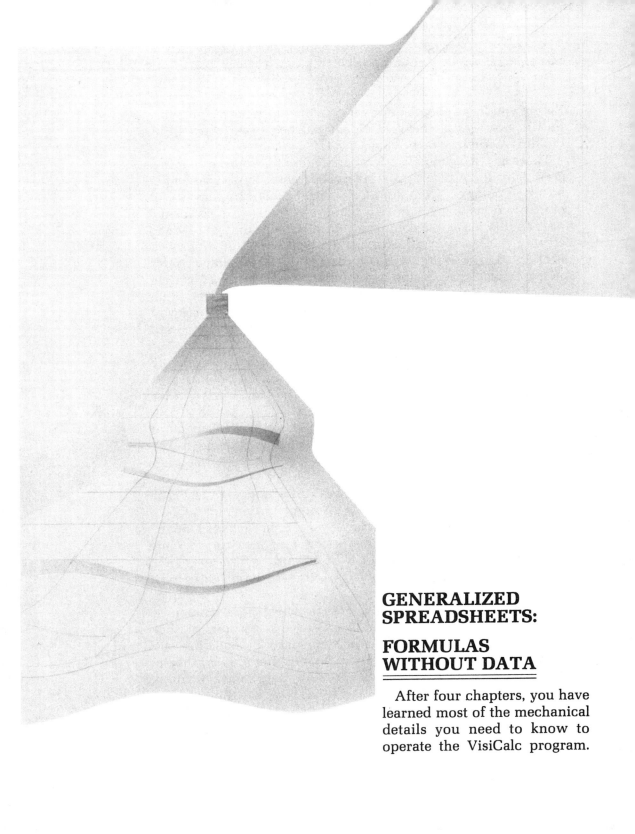

GENERALIZED SPREADSHEETS:

FORMULAS WITHOUT DATA

After four chapters, you have learned most of the mechanical details you need to know to operate the VisiCalc program.

Before you forge ahead, however, you should reflect for a while on the *structure* of the VisiCalc spreadsheets that you will be building. Structure is the subject of this chapter.

There are two general approaches to computer programming. (Yes, using the VisiCalc program *can* be classed loosely under the term computer programming. You can think of a program as a set of instructions that you give the computer in order to perform a task. In this sense, the commands and formulas that you type to create a VisiCalc spreadsheet constitute a program.) One approach is oriented toward immediate needs and quick solutions. Under this approach, you design a computer program—or a VisiCalc spreadsheet—to use only once for solving the problem at hand. You have no intention of saving this program for future use; you simply need the answer to a question, *fast*, and your only goal is to find that answer.

This approach, while intentionally short-sighted, occasionally has its place in computer use. Much more often, though, as you find yourself using a computer to perform the same kinds of tasks day in and day out, a second, more generalized approach to programming will be clearly more useful. This approach is more challenging, and, in the short term, more time-consuming. But in the long run, it is much more effective, and can save you hours—days, weeks—of programming time.

The key to this second approach is to think always in terms of creating permanent tools, rather than simply solving immediate problems. You can see right away why this approach is so tough. Under the pressure of meeting day-to-day deadlines in a work environment, it's often hard to think very far into the future—even if you *know* that working for a few extra minutes on a job today may save you an hour tomorrow.

Experience is finally what convinces most programmers—including personal computer users—of the wisdom of this approach. After you've written the same program five different times to accommodate five slightly different situations, you begin to realize that what you need is a more general approach. Writing one program that can be used many times means that in the long run you can forget about the details of the program itself, and concentrate instead on the data you are feeding the program and the answers it is giving you. It also means that *you* will be controlling the computer, rather than the other way around.

This discussion of the two approaches to programming applies as clearly to the VisiCalc program as to any other kind of programming tool. In VisiCalc, the most obvious way to generalize a spreadsheet—that is, to make it reusable—is to design a structure that is independent of the data that you will eventually feed into it. In other words, you should design spreadsheets so that you can easily change essential input data and subsequently observe the resulting changes in calculated data. This kind of design requires some thoughtful advance planning—perhaps with pencil and paper—before you begin entering the spreadsheet instructions. You should build formulas primarily with value references, rather than numerical data. While formulas are likely to remain unchanged for as long as you use a given spreadsheet, data is very likely to change. If all the data values are shown as value references, it will be very easy for you to revise your spreadsheet for new data.

We touched briefly on this point in Chapter 2. You may recall that we generalized the salesperson spreadsheet by creating a small separate table of salary-and-commission information. Then when we made changes in this data we could easily see what happened to the salary column.

The VisiCalc program offers several special features that are designed to encourage this generalized spreadsheet structure. These features include four functions—@NA, @ERROR, @ISNA, and @ISERROR—and two important, but somewhat subtle, global commands—/GO, and /GR. We will study all of these features in this chapter. In addition, to illustrate the concepts of generalized structure, we will set up a short spreadsheet that uses the @NPV function. We will discuss the meaning of net present value, and its use in business models. Figure 5.1 summarizes the five new functions we will learn about in this chapter.

THE @NA FUNCTION
AND THE /GR COMMAND

Often a spreadsheet will contain a few data values that define, or help to define, part or all of the remaining contents of the spreadsheet. This was the case in the salesperson spreadsheet, where the base salary and the commission rate determined the contents of the salary column. We sometimes call these essential values *parameters*. When we isolate these values somewhere on the spreadsheet in a special table complete with labels, we can refer to that space on the spreadsheet as the *parameter table*. The parameter table, then, is the location where you store or revise the defining data of a spreadsheet; to see the *results* of these values, you look elsewhere on the spreadsheet.

At some point during your use of a spreadsheet, some or all of the parameter values may be unavailable. Or, you may wish to leave all the values of the parameter table blank while you develop the formulas. For these instances, the VisiCalc program supplies the @NA function. @NA, which stands for Not Available, is a function that requires no arguments. If you enter @NA into a

Function	Arguments	Description
@NA	none	Displays the message NA (for Not Available) in a spreadsheet position. If a position displaying NA is used as a value reference in a formula, then the result of the formula will also be NA.
@ISNA	value	Returns a value of true if the value reference in its argument is NA; otherwise, returns false.
@ERROR	none	Displays the message ERROR in a position; if a position displaying ERROR is used as a value reference in a formula, then the result of the formula will also be ERROR.
@ISERROR	value	Returns a value of true if the value reference in its argument displays ERROR; otherwise, returns false.
@NPV	value, range	Using the value argument as the *discount rate*, finds the *net present value* of the values in the range; the discount rate must be expressed as a decimal, not a percentage.

Figure 5.1: Miscellaneous Functions

position on the spreadsheet, VisiCalc simply displays the message:

NA

in that position. But even more to the point, if you write a formula that contains a value reference to a position whose current contents are NA, the result of the formula will *also* be displayed as NA.

Let's try a simple experiment to see how this works. We'll place a value in position A1, and a percentage in position A2. In A3 we'll write a formula to multiply the value by the percentage:

+A1*(A2/100)

Start out by entering a random value—say, 450—into position A1. Then move the cursor to A2, but instead of typing a value, enter the function @NA. Notice on the contents line that VisiCalc accepts this as a value:

A2 (V) @NA

Next move the cursor to position A3 and enter the formula shown above. Study the results. The contents line shows the formula correctly, but the position itself displays NA. Here's what your spreadsheet should look like:

A3 (V) +A1 * (A2/100)

```
        A
1      450
2      NA
3      NA
```

VisiCalc is ready to compute the result of the formula at A3 whenever you provide a value for A2. But until then, since the formula depends on the data at A2, the result will be shown as NA.

Enter the value 10 at position A2 and watch what happens. A value is immediately calculated from the formula at A3:

```
        A
1      450
2       10
3       45
```

You can see how the @NA function could be valuable in the development of a generalized spreadsheet. When you establish a parameter table, you can initially give all of the parameters values of @NA. Then you can proceed with writing the formulas of your spreadsheet as though the parameter table already had values. The result of any formulas that reference the values of the parameter table will simply appear as NA.

To illustrate the @NA function in a more significant way, we're going to begin building a short spreadsheet for studying the future income from investments. This spreadsheet will eventually contain three distinct sections of data—a parameter table, a range of intermediate yearly values, and a pair of entries that summarize the total value of the investment. The third section is actually the "bottom line"—the answer to the question, *What is this investment worth?*

The parameter table will start out with three values: the date of the first year of the investment project (for example, 1983), the expected amount of income during the first year, and the expected yearly percent increase or decrease in income over subsequent years of the project. All these values will start out as NA:

FIRST YEAR OF PROJECT	NA
INCOME DURING NA	NA
YEARLY % CHANGE	NA

In this spreadsheet we will examine the income from the investment for five years into the future. In the following paragraphs we'll go through the development of this spreadsheet step by step.

To lay the foundation of the spreadsheet, we'll execute two global commands and draw lines to separate the various sections of information. One of the clear advantages of planning ahead like this is that "housekeeping" tasks can be taken care of all at once, and so take less time. To begin, then, type in the following sequence of commands:

```
/GC7              {decrease column width to 7 spaces}
/GF$              {global dollar-and-cent format}
>A1 /—=           {draw lines for the spreadsheet}
>A3 /—=
>A10 /—=
>A13 /FR "— — — —
>A16 /—=
```

```
>A1              {go to A1 to replicate lines}
/R               {invoke replication command}
.A16 (return)    {source range: A1...A16}
B1.E1 (return)   {target range: B1...E1}
```

Figure 5.2 shows the results of these commands. The lines divide the spreadsheet into four sections—the first is for the title of the spreadsheet, then the parameter table, the yearly values, and the totals will follow. We have used the global dollar-and-cent format command on the spreadsheet, even though some of the values will not be in that format. We'll have to format nonconforming values individually.

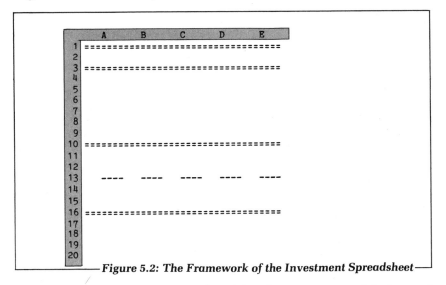

Figure 5.2: The Framework of the Investment Spreadsheet

The next step is to enter the title, the parameter labels, and @NA for the parameter values themselves. Since the column width is set at 7 spaces, we'll have to enter each label seven characters at a time; some of the labels will cross column boundaries:

```
>B2 INVESTM      {row 2: the title}
>C2 ENT SCE
>D2 NARIOS
>A5 FIRST Y      {row 5: first parameter label}
>B5 EAR OF
>C5 PROJECT
```

```
>D5 /FI @NA          {date in integer format; not available yet}
>A6 INCOME           {row 6: second parameter label}
>B6 DURING
>C6 /FI +D5          {year comes from position D5}
>D6 @NA              {parameter value not available}
>A7 YEARLY           {row 7: third parameter label}
>B7 "% CHANG
>C7 E
>D7 /FG @NA          {percent in general format; value not available}
```

Figure 5.3 shows the spreadsheet at this point in its development. The word *scenarios* in the title expresses the "what-if" nature of the spreadsheet—any given investment can be studied from different perspectives simply by making individual changes in the parameter values. Notice that all the values are expressed as NA at the moment. Look in particular at position C6; this position is actually part of the second parameter label. It will display the date of the first year, once that value is available at position D5.

Next we move to the intermediate data section. The date and the income for the first year come directly from the parameter table:

```
>A12 /FI +D5         {date of first year}
>A14 +D6             {income for first year}
```

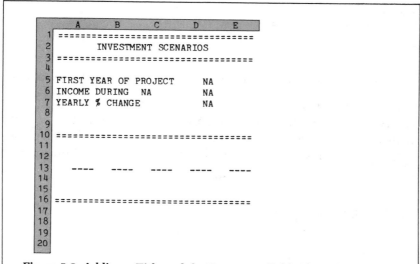

Figure 5.3: Adding a Title and the Parameter Table

Subsequent values have to be calculated and then replicated:

```
>B12 /FI +A12+1              {date incrementation}
>B14 +A14*(1+(D7/100))       {formula for yearly changes in
                              income}

>B12                         {go to B12}
/R                           {invoke replication command}
.B14 (return)                {source range: B12...B14}
C12.E12 (return)             {target range: C12...E12}
R RN                         {A12 and A14 are relative; D7
                              does not change}
```

So far, all the values display NA, as shown in Figure 5.4. Let's try entering some values into the parameter table now. Start with the year, at D5:

```
>D5 1983    {enter a date at D5}
```

As soon as you enter the date, several changes occur on the spreadsheet. The date appears in the parameter label in row 6, and a series of five incrementing dates appears in row 12. These are all the values that depend on the parameter value at position D5.

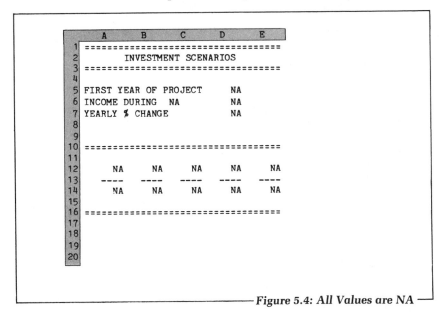

Figure 5.4: All Values are NA

Now enter a value for the first year's income and a percentage value for the change. (We'll assume once again that the monetary values are in units of $1,000.):

>D6 23.7   {first year's income: $23,700}

>D7 8.5   {yearly percent change: 8.5%}

Changes occur on the spreadsheet after *each* value entry. The final result is shown in Figure 5.5.

You can easily investigate variations of this investment. What if the yearly increase were only 7.8%—what would the income be in 1987? To find out, move the cursor to position D7, enter the new parameter value 7.8, and observe the result. The new calculated income for 1987 is 32.01 (or, $32,010).

Sometimes you'll want to change more than one parameter value at a time. For example, what if the first-year's income is only $19,500, and the yearly increase is 9%? As you enter each of these new values onto the parameter table, you notice that the table is recalculated after *each* new entry. But you are actually only interested in a single new calculation—after *both* new values have been entered.

On this particular spreadsheet, the time difference between re-calculating only once and recalculating twice is small. But imagine a more complicated spreadsheet, with a larger parameter table

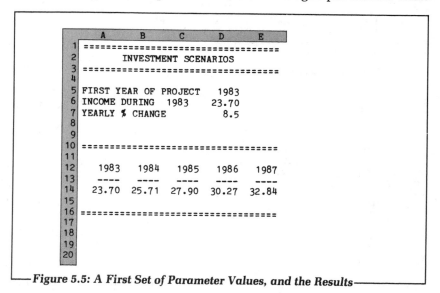

Figure 5.5: A First Set of Parameter Values, and the Results

and more complex formulas. You may have to wait seconds, or even minutes, for the VisiCalc program to carry out the recalculations. This would be inconvenient if you had, say, six or so new parameter values to enter onto the table. Waiting for a complete recalculation of the spreadsheet six different times would mean a considerable delay. It would be much more convenient if you could prevent the VisiCalc program from performing a recalculation until you had entered all six of the new values.

This is where the global recalculation command, /GR, becomes valuable. The VisiCalc program has two modes of recalculation—automatic and manual. When you first load the VisiCalc program from disk and start it running on your computer, it is in the automatic recalculation mode. This means that each time you enter a new value, the *entire* spreadsheet is automatically recalculated. You can switch to the manual mode (or back again to automatic) using the global recalculation command.

Type /GR and look at the message on the prompt line:

    RECALC: A M

A is for automatic; M for manual. You are currently in the automatic mode, so type M to switch to the manual mode. Notice that there is no visible change on the screen when you do this; you have to remember which recalculation mode you are in at any given moment.

Now let's change all three values of the parameter table. Enter these values:

    >D5 1984
    >D6 35.75
    >D7 8.2

Notice that no changes occur in the calculated data of the spreadsheet as you enter these new values. All the dates and the yearly income figures are unchanged from the previous scenario. This is because you have to *force* recalculation when you are in the manual recalculation mode. The way you do this is by typing the exclamation mark character (!) on your keyboard when you are ready to see the results of the new parameter values.

Try it. Type ! and watch all the new calculated values appear at once. Your new spreadsheet should look like Figure 5.6.

To summarize, we have seen two tools for developing generalized spreadsheets. The @NA function allows you to distinguish the process of creating formulas from the process of entering data into those formulas. The /GRM command is a way of streamlining the recalculation process when you have many parameter changes for a new scenario. Recalculation occurs only when you request it by typing !. (You can always return to the automatic recalculation mode by entering the /GRA command.)

We should add one last note about the @NA function. You may occasionally have "optional" entries in your parameter tables—that is, values that appear in some scenarios, but remain unavailable—for whatever reason—in others. In this case, the fact that a value is not available is a significant piece of information for your spreadsheet. In other words, the entry NA is actually a *value* that you would like to be able to recognize in the logic of your spreadsheet.

The VisiCalc program comes through once again with an answer to this need. The @ISNA function returns a value of true or false, depending on whether or not its argument is NA. Typically the argument of @ISNA will be a value reference and the function itself will be used in an @IF statement:

```
@IF(@ISNA(D8),(value#1),(value#2))
```

If @ISNA returns a true, then value #1 is chosen; if it returns a false, then value #2.

You may encounter situations where the unavailability of a piece

```
        A         B         C         D         E
 1 ===================================
 2         INVESTMENT SCENARIOS
 3 ===================================
 4
 5 FIRST YEAR OF PROJECT    1984
 6 INCOME DURING  1984     35.75
 7 YEARLY % CHANGE           8.2
 8
 9
10 ===================================
11
12    1984    1985    1986    1987    1988
13    ----    ----    ----    ----    ----
14   35.75   38.68   41.85   45.29   49.00
15
16 ===================================
17
18
19
20
```

Figure 5.6: Forced Recalculation in the Manual Recalculation Mode

of data takes on a significance of its own. For these instances, @ISNA will prove valuable.

We still have a third section to add to our investment spreadsheet. As we do so, we'll learn something about the way VisiCalc performs calculations, and we'll discover a subtle—but easily remedied—flaw in our spreadsheet design.

THE /GO COMMAND

Row 18 on the spreadsheet will be the total earnings line:

    >A18 TOTAL E   {total earnings label}

    >B18 ARNINGS

In position D18, type the formula for finding the sum of the yearly income figures:

    >D18 @SUM(A14.E14)   {summation formula}

The value 210.57 (meaning $210,570) will appear in position D18.

Now let's see what happens when we change one of the values of the parameter table. Go to position D7, and change the yearly percent change to 10 (for 10%). Type ! to force a recalculation. The yearly income figures all change accordingly, and a new value appears for the total. (The result is shown in Figure 5.7.)

But something is wrong. The row of yearly income figures has not been added correctly. The value in position D18 should be

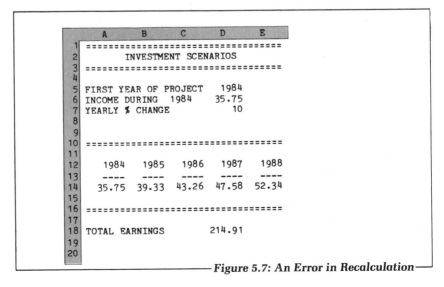

Figure 5.7: An Error in Recalculation

218.26. Instead, the position displays the value 214.91. Has the VisiCalc program failed us?

No, it hasn't; we merely have yet to learn one of its characteristics. Recall back in Chapter 1 when we first examined the information presented on the VisiCalc screen. We made note of the C in the upper right corner. This C stands for column, which is the *order of calculation* mode in which VisiCalc begins. We've pretty much ignored this message since then, because the issue has never come up before.

In the column order mode, the VisiCalc program recalculates the spreadsheet in the following order: it begins with position A1, recalculates all the values in column A, then moves to B1, recalculates column B, and so on. Up to now this order of recalculation has never caused us problems on our spreadsheets.

In the investment spreadsheet, however, we have discovered a discrepancy between our *concept* of the order of recalculation, and the *reality* of VisiCalc's method. Look again at Figure 5.7 to see exactly what happened. When we entered a new percentage rate at position D7, what we were expecting was that VisiCalc would recalculate all five of the yearly income figures, and then find the sum of these new figures for the total earnings entry. What actually happened was this: VisiCalc recalculated each whole column, one column at a time. When it arrived at column D, it first recalculated the new income for 1987 (position D14) and then the total earnings (position D18). But at this point position E14, in column E, still contained the *old* income value for 1988 (i.e., from the previous scenario). So the incorrect total earnings figure was based on four new yearly values, and one old yearly value.

The VisiCalc program was working by columns; we had conceptualized our spreadsheet by rows. The flaw in our planning caused the error.

You've undoubtedly guessed the point of all this by now: in some cases, you have to be aware of VisiCalc's order of recalculation, and make sure that you either plan your spreadsheet to match that order, or change the order to correspond with your spreadsheet. The way to change the order of calculation is via the /GO command.

When you type /GO, you'll see this message on the prompt line:

REEVAL ORDER: R C

To make VisiCalc calculate by rows, type R. When you do so, you'll see the letter in the upper-right corner of the screen change to R. Thanks to this message, you always know which order mode the VisiCalc program is in—R for row, or C for column.

Type the ! character. The correct value for the total earnings—218.26—will appear in position D18. Now try making some additional changes in the parameter values. You will see that all the values are calculated correctly now that the VisiCalc program is in the row order mode.

An alternative approach would have been to force recalculation twice, while the program was in the column order mode. Once the correct yearly income values had been determined, a second recalculation of the spreadsheet would have arrived at the correct total value for the five years of investment. Sometimes you may need to force recalculation more than once, if you design very complicated spreadsheets. The best design is the simplest design, however. You should decide—at the time you plan your spreadsheet—which order mode will be appropriate. You should also try to avoid using too many value references that go forward across the lines of recalculation. As we have seen in this example, *forward references* can cause trouble if you're not aware of them.

The last line that we'll include on the investment spreadsheet is for the *net present value* of the investment. This value is essential for comparing different investment scenarios.

THE NET PRESENT VALUE

Present value calculations are simply a way of accounting for the time-value of money. The fact that money has value over time is an every-day reality. It explains why you earn interest when you put money in a bank account and why you *pay* interest when you take out a loan. Over time, money can be put to work to earn more money. Thus, the dollar you have in your pocket today is more valuable to you than a dollar that you know you will receive a year from today; you can put today's dollar to work for you during the year that you're waiting for the second dollar. (There may also be other, economic, reasons why today's dollar is more valuable; but these reasons are not involved in the discussion at hand.)

Present value, then, is a way of expressing how much a known future income is worth to you today. For example, let's say you know that you will inherit $1000 in five years. Meanwhile, you have a bank account right now that earns you a total of 6% interest per year on your money. You calculate that if you put $747 in your account today, it would be worth $1000—the amount of your inheritance—in five years. Likewise, you can say that the present value of your future inheritance, at a 6% *discount rate*, is $747.

The *net present value* of a series of future income amounts is simply the sum of their present values. The arithmetic of finding the net present value depends on three factors—the amount of the future income, the number of years until you expect to earn it, and the discount rate you use. This calculation can be messy and time consuming if you have to perform it by hand. VisiCalc's @NPV function performs it for you painlessly. The form of the net present value function is:

>   @NPV(value, range)

The value argument represents the discount rate. It must be expressed as a decimal, not a percentage. The range argument represents the range of future values.

So, to incorporate the net present value onto your spreadsheet, first add the discount rate to the parameter table at row 8:

>   >A8 DISCOUN   {row 8: new parameter label}
>   >B8 T RATE
>   >D8 /FG @NA   {general format; value not available yet}

Then enter the label and the formula for the net present value:

>   >A19 NET PRE   {net present value label}
>   >B19 SENT VA
>   >C19 LUE
>   >D19 @NPV(D8/100,A14.E14)   {net present value formula}

So that you can enter the discount rate as a percentage at position D8, the value is divided by 100 in the @NPV formula at D19. At the moment both positions D8 and D19 display NA.

Let's say you intend to use a 12% discount rate for the calculation. Move the cursor to D8, enter the value 12, and type ! to force a recalculation. The value 154.00 appears at position D19. (See Figure 5.8.) The net present value of this particular investment, then, is $154,000. Notice that this figure is considerably less than the total earnings of $218,260.

```
            A        B        C        D        E
  1  ====================================
  2         INVESTMENT  SCENARIOS
  3  ====================================
  4
  5  FIRST YEAR OF PROJECT     1984
  6  INCOME DURING  1984      35.75
  7  YEARLY % CHANGE             10
  8  DISCOUNT RATE               12
  9
 10  ====================================
 11
 12     1984     1985     1986     1987     1988
 13     ----     ----     ----     ----     ----
 14    35.75    39.33    43.26    47.58    52.34
 15
 16  ====================================
 17
 18  TOTAL EARNINGS           218.26
 19  NET PRESENT VALUE        154.00
 20
```

Figure 5.8: The Net Present Value Calculation

THE @ERROR AND @ISERROR FUNCTIONS

We can add one more feature to the investment spreadsheet to make the parameter table even more reliable. Many times when you include a value in a parameter table, it will be important to make sure the value falls between specified upper and lower limits. For example, in the case of a percentage, you may want the value to be greater than 0 and less than 100. When you type data into a parameter table, there is always the danger that you may inadvertently enter an inappropriate value, which would make the results inaccurate and useless.

You can use the VisiCalc @ERROR function, combined with the @IF statement, to print an error message directly onto the spreadsheet if an inappropriate value appears on the parameter table. The @ERROR function, which requires no argument, simply displays the word:

ERROR

in the position where it is entered. (You may have already noticed that the VisiCalc program itself also prints this message on occasion. Usually this happens when you enter a command or some data that VisiCalc can't understand—for example, when you use a function incorrectly, or type an unintelligible formula, or enter some illegal arithmetic, such as division by zero.)

Since we are likely to want the discount rate at position D8 to be a value greater than zero and less than 100, we can expand the net present value formula (D19) so that ERROR will appear if the discount rate is outside the correct range:

>D19 @IF(@AND(D8<100,D8>0),@NPV(D8/100,A14.E14),@ERROR)

This function says: If the discount rate (at D8) is less than 100 and greater than zero, calculate the net present value; otherwise, display ERROR at position D19. Try it out by entering a number at D8 that is outside the correct range, say 105. Type! to force the recalculation. You will see the ERROR message at D19.

This kind of input error checking is another element of good program design—in VisiCalc, or any other programming tool. Your spreadsheets will be more reliable if you can assure accuracy of input parameter values.

VisiCalc also has an @ISERROR function, similar to the @ISNA function; you can use it whenever it is important to check for an error condition before proceeding with a calculation. Like @ISNA, it returns a true or a false value—true if its value reference argument contains the value ERROR, otherwise, false.

EXAMINING "SCENARIOS"

You now have in front of you a short, but complete, spreadsheet that you can use to compare the value of different five-year investment projects. The net present value is the specific tool that you will use for the comparison.

Let us say that you have three investment possibilities to choose from, and each begins in 1983. All of them require the same amount of initial investment capital, so you can eliminate that value as a factor in the comparison.

- From project #1 you can expect an income of $36,500 the first year; for each of the four following years, the amount of return is expected to *decrease* by 10%.
- Project #2 will return $16,000 the first year and a 32% increase in return each of the following years.
- Project #3 will return $30,000 for each of the five years of the investment.

You know that the total income from each of the investments is approximately $150,000, but you would like to compare the net present value of the three projects. You are using a discount rate of 12% for the present value calculation.

Figures 5.9, 5.10, and 5.11 show the three investments worked

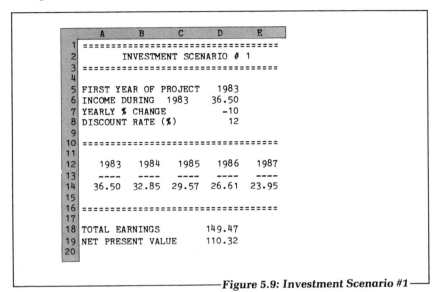

Figure 5.9: Investment Scenario #1

Figure 5.10: Investment Scenario #2

```
        A       B       C       D       E
 1  =====================================
 2          INVESTMENT  SCENARIO  # 3
 3  =====================================
 4
 5  FIRST YEAR OF PROJECT    1983
 6  INCOME DURING   1983     30.00
 7  YEARLY % CHANGE             0
 8  DISCOUNT RATE (%)          12
 9
10  =====================================
11
12     1983    1984    1985    1986    1987
13     ----    ----    ----    ----    ----
14    30.00   30.00   30.00   30.00   30.00
15
16  =====================================
17
18  TOTAL EARNINGS           150.00
19  NET PRESENT VALUE        108.14
20
```

Figure 5.11: Investment Scenario #3

out on the investment spreadsheet. (Notice that the title of the spreadsheet has been revised slightly to identify the different scenarios.) In each case only two new parameter values had to be entered—the first year's income and the yearly percent change—and then a recalculation was forced. You should create these three scenario spreadsheets, and save each one on disk. We will be using them again in Chapter 6.

Figure 5.12 shows a summary of the three investments. With a

```
        A       B       C       D
 1  ===================================
 2         INVESTMENT  SCENARIOS
 3  ===================================
 4             #1      #2      #3
 5             ==      ==      ==
 6
 7  FIRST YR.  36.50   16.00   30.00
 8  % CHANGE   -10     32       0
 9  DISC RATE   12     12      12
10
11  ===================================
12
13  TOTAL      149.47  150.37  150.00
14  NPV        110.32  101.92  108.14
15
16  ===================================
```

Figure 5.12: Summary of the Investment Scenarios

net present value of $110,320, investment #1 appears to be the most valuable of the three projects, even though the actual total income is slightly less than from the other two investments.

SUMMARY

If you design the structure of your spreadsheets carefully, you can create tools that will prove to be of continuing value, rather than just one-time use. The main principle to keep in mind is that specific data tends to change from scenario to scenario, but formulas generally remain the same. The *parameter table* is a structure that is ideally suited to generalized spreadsheets.

The VisiCalc program itself provides several features that are important in this context. The @NA function is useful during the development of a spreadsheet. It allows you to concentrate on writing formulas without worrying about data. The /GRM command puts recalculation into a manual mode, so that you can change as many parameter values as you want without having to wait for irrelevant recalculations after each change. In this mode you specify the correct moment for recalculation by typing the ! character.

Understanding exactly how the VisiCalc program recalculates spreadsheets is essential to assuring accuracy and reliability, especially when the network of value references becomes complicated in a spreadsheet. VisiCalc can recalculate either by columns or by rows, but it is your responsibility to plan your spreadsheet around one or the other order mode. The /GO command changes the order mode. A letter (C or R) in the upper-right corner of the VisiCalc screen shows you which mode you are in at any given moment.

A final element of good spreadsheet design is data input error checking for the values of a parameter table. The @ERROR function can be used to display an error message right on the spreadsheet in the event of an input error.

CHAPTER SIX

DIF FILES, PART I: AN INTRODUCTION

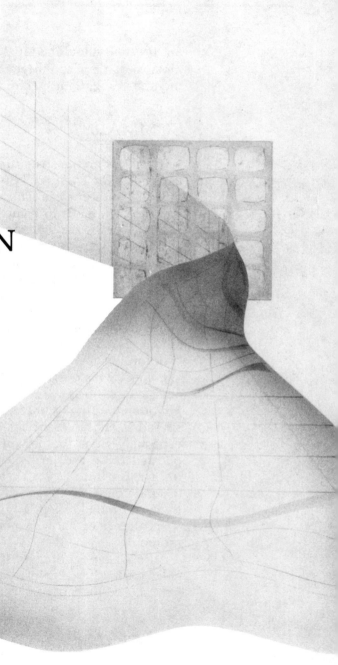

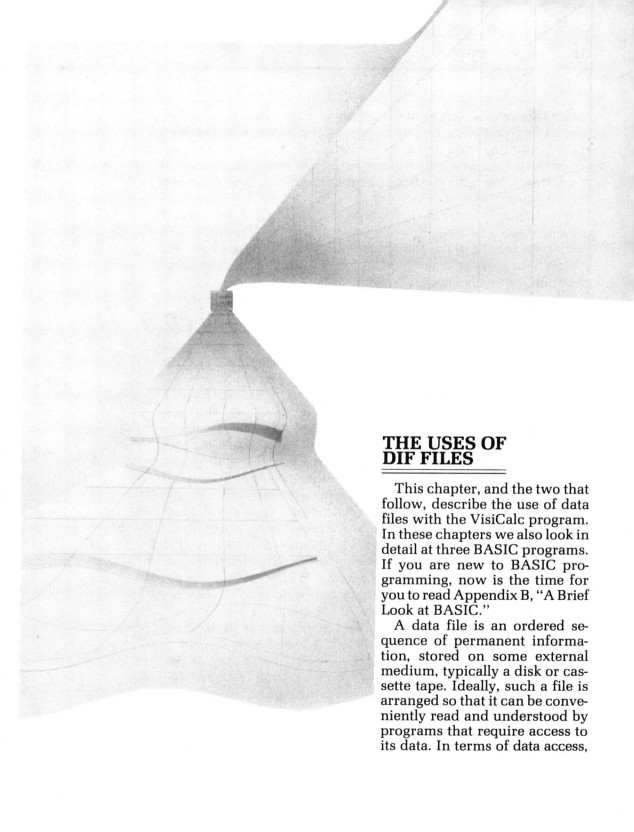

THE USES OF DIF FILES

This chapter, and the two that follow, describe the use of data files with the VisiCalc program. In these chapters we also look in detail at three BASIC programs. If you are new to BASIC programming, now is the time for you to read Appendix B, "A Brief Look at BASIC."

A data file is an ordered sequence of permanent information, stored on some external medium, typically a disk or cassette tape. Ideally, such a file is arranged so that it can be conveniently read and understood by programs that require access to its data. In terms of data access, there are two categories of data files: *sequential* data files, which must be read (or written) in a very specific order—starting from the beginning, and moving forward, data item by data item; and *random access* files, which allow the data to be read or revised in any order. We will be talking about sequential files in these last three chapters.

We might compare the two kinds of files to a mystery novel and a dictionary, respectively—one you read from beginning to end without ever breaking the sequential order, and the other you refer to in random order, depending on your needs for the information it provides.

The purpose of a data file is to provide an *independent* medium for storing information. Independent from what? From two things: First, independent from the events that occur on your computer itself, and second, independent from the programs that create and use the information stored in the file. Since a data file is stored on an external memory medium, the data is safe even when you turn your computer off. If you use a program to create a data file today, you can return to that file tomorrow with confidence that the information will still be there. A data file may be used by different programs that perform distinct tasks. Data files may even be read by different *kinds* of programs, so that programs written in different languages can exchange information with one another. For this kind of exchange to take place successfully, however, the data file must be arranged in a carefully defined format. Each program that uses the file must "know" the format.

The Data Interchange Format, DIF, is one such format. It is designed for storing VisiCalc data and for sharing that data with other programs. The VisiCalc program can both read and create files in the DIF format. This format is also designed to be conveniently read (or written) by BASIC programs.

DIF files contain two different kinds of information. First, there is the actual data that the file has been created to store. Second, every DIF file is *self-documenting*. That is, the file contains information *about itself*. For example, one section of the DIF file tells you how many data items the file contains, and how they are arranged. In addition, DIF files have a system for telling you the *type*—numeric or nonnumeric—of each data item. All this information is arranged in a simple, reliable, and perfectly predictable format.

It is important to keep in mind the difference between a DIF file and a VisiCalc spreadsheet file. A spreadsheet file contains all the information that you enter into the VisiCalc program to create a given spreadsheet. This information includes formats, formulas, and global commands, in addition to the labels and values themselves. In other words, a spreadsheet file contains everything the VisiCalc program needs to know in order to duplicate completely a spreadsheet that you have created. You have probably been creating many spreadsheet files as you have progressed through this book. They are created using the /SS command. We have been labeling them with the suffix ".VC" to make it clear what kind of files they are.

These VisiCalc spreadsheet files are private to the VisiCalc program; that is, they are not designed to be used by other kinds of programs. A DIF file, on the other hand, contains only the information that you are likely to want to pass from VisiCalc to, say, a BASIC program. You would certainly not be interested in using VisiCalc formulas or commands in BASIC. None of these VisiCalc elements would be intelligible in the BASIC language. However, you might well be interested in transferring *data*—labels and values from a VisiCalc spreadsheet—to a BASIC program. Say, for example, you are writing a BASIC program designed to process data in a way that is inconvenient—or impossible—in VisiCalc, but the source of this data, and then the ultimate destination, is a VisiCalc spreadsheet. (We will see such programs in the chapters ahead.) Your means of transporting the data from the VisiCalc spreadsheet to your BASIC program, and then back again, is a DIF file.

So, a DIF file contains the *data* from a VisiCalc spreadsheet, but not the formulas or commands used to create and format the data. DIF files, as you will soon see for yourself, are created by the /S# command.

In these last three chapters we will be concentrating on the use of DIF files for transferring spreadsheet data between VisiCalc and BASIC. There is, however, a second important use of DIF files; it is for moving rows and columns of data (again, *not* formulas or formats) from one spreadsheet to another, within the VisiCalc program. This second use does *not* require that you know anything about the DIF format itself. VisiCalc takes care of all the details of the data transfer automatically.

The last spreadsheet shown in Chapter 5—the summary of the three investment scenarios (Figure 5.12)—was created using DIF files to transfer data from the scenario spreadsheets (Figures 5.9, 5.10, and 5.11). Before we begin talking about the structure of DIF files and their use in BASIC programs, let's examine this simpler—but still very valuable—use of DIF.

TRANSFERRING DATA
BETWEEN SPREADSHEETS

If you saved the three investment scenarios on disk, then you can follow along through the steps required for creating the summary spreadsheet. You'll recall that the parameter values (date, yearly income, percent change, and discount rate) and the calculated totals (total earnings, and net present value) all appeared in column D of these three spreadsheets. This was good planning; as a result we can create a summary spreadsheet simply by transferring a single column from each of the investment spreadsheets.

We'll begin with investment scenario #1 (Figure 5.9). Use the /SL command to load the spreadsheet onto your VisiCalc screen from your disk. Move the cursor to position D5. This position contains the date of the first year of the investment; it is also the top of the column of values that you want to transfer. Now type the DIF file storage command: /S#. On the prompt line you will see:

    DATA: SAVE LOAD

You respond to this command by typing S or L, depending on whether you want to *save* data as a DIF file or *load* data from a DIF file. In this example, type an S, for save. The next prompt is:

    DATA SAVE: FILE FOR SAVING

At this point you have to type a file name for the DIF file that you are about to create. Use the name:

    INV1.DIF

for "investment scenario #1." Notice the suffix ".DIF". This is important. You may end up saving many different files on one disk, and eventually it will be hard to tell them all apart unless you give them names that clearly identify their contents and their file types. Just as we used ".VC" to identify a VisiCalc spreadsheet file, now we'll use ".DIF" consistently to identify DIF files. (Some versions of VisiCalc automatically supply this suffix when you use the /S# command. Otherwise, if you have a version that does not supply it, you'll have to type the suffix in yourself.)

Once you have entered the file name, your disk drive will be active for a moment, and then you'll see yet another prompt on the screen:

DATA SAVE: LOWER RIGHT

A DIF file will store any *rectangular* portion of your spreadsheet—from the contents of a single position, up to many rows or columns of data. When you use the /S# command, you define the rectangle of data as follows: the *upper-left* corner of the rectangle is defined as the position of the cursor at the time you type /S# (D5 in this case). You indicate the *lower-right* corner of the rectangle when VisiCalc prompts you for it. As usual, you can either type the address of the position, or you can move the cursor to the position, and then press return.

In this example, since our "rectangle" consists of a single column of data, the lower-right corner of the rectangle is position D19. Enter this address. You'll then see one last prompt that you must answer before the DIF file will be created:

DATA SAVE: R, C OR RETURN

This prompt is asking you whether you want to save your data by rows or by columns. (R or return saves by rows; C saves by columns.) When you are simply saving DIF files to transfer data to another spreadsheet, your choice between row and column storage is not very important, *as long as you remember which way you did store the data.* (The choice will be more important later, when we prepare DIF files for BASIC programs.) For now, type a C to save the data as a column. When you do so, your disk drive will activate, storing the file.

You should follow this same sequence of instructions for each of the remaining two investment scenarios. Call the second DIF file:

INV2.DIF

and the third:

INV3.DIF

To make the job easier, here is a summary of the commands you must give to store the files correctly. First clear the screen and load the VisiCalc investment file. Then enter the following sequence of instructions:

>D5	{move the cursor to D5}
/S#	{invoke the DIF storage command}
S	{to **save** a DIF file}
INV2.DIF (return)	{enter the name of the file}
D19 (return)	{lower-right corner of rectangle}
C	{to save by **columns**}

When you have saved all three DIF files in this way, you are ready to create the summary spreadsheet. Clear the screen. With the cursor at position A1, type the following commands:

/S#	{invoke the DIF storage command}
L	{to **load** a DIF file}
INV1.DIF (return)	{enter the file name}
C	{to load by **columns**}

Since you saved the DIF files by columns, you must also load them by columns if you want them to appear in the same direction on the summary spreadsheet. Now use the same commands to load INV2.DIF into column B and INV3.DIF into column C. The resulting spreadsheet is shown in Figure 6.1.

In its initial form, this spreadsheet looks unusual; you may barely recognize it as the basis for the investment summary spreadsheet. Of course, you know by now that it will only take a few short steps to transform the spreadsheet. You'll begin by deleting the rows of irrelevant data, using /DR. For example, the

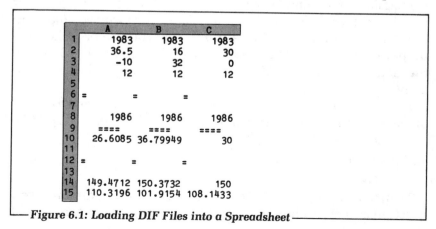

Figure 6.1: Loading DIF Files into a Spreadsheet

investment return of 1986, which appeared in column D of each of the original scenario spreadsheets, is not needed for the summary spreadsheet. After you have deleted the unwanted rows, you'll quickly reformat the data (/GF$, and then /FI for each of the dates and percentages). Finally, you'll insert rows and columns for a title; labels for the columns and rows; and lines across the spreadsheet to improve the presentation. These steps will result in the spreadsheet you saw at the end of Chapter 5.

But before you do any of this, take a moment to study the spreadsheet in its raw form, just back from the DIF files. You can learn a lot about DIF files by examining the data that they return to your spreadsheet.

First, move the cursor around the spreadsheet and watch the contents line at the top of the screen. At no point does the contents line display the *formulas* that were used to create the data. It only displays the data itself. This, of course, illustrates what we have already said about DIF files—they store data, not formulas. When you create a DIF file, the file merely stores the *current contents* of the rectangle you indicate on the spreadsheet. The formulas that created those contents are irrelevant to DIF.

Next, notice the format of the numerical data. The values appear in the *general* format. All the calculated values are displayed on the contents line with several decimal places of accuracy. These values were in the dollar-and-cent format on the investment scenario spreadsheets. But DIF does *not* record this original format. A DIF file records all numeric data values in the *general* data format.

Finally, look at what became of the lines in rows 6 and 12. You may recall that these lines were created with the repeating label command, /–. DIF cannot record the *results* of the repeating label command. Rather, it only stores the character (or characters) that you entered for repetition. In this case the character was the equal sign.

Now, for practice, go ahead and transform the raw spreadsheet into a presentable summary spreadsheet. Delete lines 6 to 12, reformat the data, and insert the labels and lines. The whole job should take only a few minutes.

One last point about transferring data between spreadsheets: If you wish to transform a row of data into a column, you can do so by using a DIF file. The method is simple. Save the data as a column and then load it back as a row, or vice versa. Try it with the file INV1.DIF. Clear the screen and type the DIF storage command, /S#. Load the file, but in response to the prompt:

DATA LOAD: R, C OR RETURN

type R instead of C. You will see your data appear on the screen as a row.

THE RAINFALL SPREADSHEET

Throughout the remainder of this chapter, and in Chapters 7 and 8, we will be dealing with a single DIF file. You'll recall that back in Chapter 1 we began with a table of unlabeled numbers, and then we imagined three possible applications for the numbers. We have followed up on the first two applications—resulting in the home grocery expense spreadsheet and the salesperson spreadsheet. Now we are ready to take up the third—the rainfall spreadsheet, which is shown in Figure 6.2. It shows the average monthly precipitation for ten U.S. cities.

We will assume that you have the following data processing requirements for this spreadsheet:

1. The spreadsheet will eventually have to expand to include more cities; therefore, any tasks that you perform must be independent of the size of the table.

2. You want to calculate some statistical values from the data. For starters, you need to compute the *variance* and the *standard deviation* for the monthly precipitation figures of each city.

3. You require the capability to *sort* the spreadsheet data in either of two ways—alphabetically, by the names of the cities (column A), or numerically, by the total precipitation (column N, in descending order).

We will see how we can satisfy all these requirements by following three basic steps: storing the data in a DIF file; writing BASIC programs to read the file and perform the special processing tasks; and finally, in the case of the sorting operation, creating a new DIF file to return the data to VisiCalc. But before we begin any of this, we must examine the nature of the Data Interchange Format.

Specifically, we will look at a DIF file of the rainfall spreadsheet to find out exactly how DIF is organized.

Create a copy of the rainfall spreadsheet for your own use. Begin by loading the raw data, from the file NUMBERS.VC, into your VisiCalc program. Use the /GFI command to format all the numbers on your spreadsheet as integers. Insert a column at the left (/IC) and five rows at the top (/IR, five times), and enter the title, the labels, and the lines as shown in Figure 6.2.

Now you are ready to create the DIF file for this spreadsheet.

	A	B	C	D	E	F	G
1				MONTHLY NORMAL PRECIPITATION			
2				(IN CENTIMETERS)			
3	==						
4		JAN	FEB	MAR	APR	MAY	JUN
5		===	===	===	===	===	===
6	HONOLULU	11	6	8	4	3	1
7	LOS ANGL	8	7	6	3	0	0
8	SAN FRAN	11	8	6	4	1	0
9	DENVER	2	2	3	5	7	5
10	ST.LOUIS	5	5	8	10	10	11
11	NEW ORLN	11	12	14	11	11	12
12	CLEVELND	7	6	8	9	9	8
13	MIAMI	6	5	5	9	15	23
14	WASH DC	7	6	8	7	10	9
15	NEW YORK	7	7	9	8	9	8

	H	I	J	K	L	M	N
1							
2							
3	==						
4	JUL	AUG	SEP	OCT	NOV	DEC	TOTALS
5	===	===	===	===	===	===	======
6	2	2	2	4	8	9	59
7	0	0	1	1	5	6	36
8	0	0	1	3	6	10	50
9	5	3	3	3	2	1	39
10	9	7	7	7	6	5	91
11	17	13	14	6	10	13	144
12	4	8	7	7	7	6	85
13	18	17	22	21	7	4	152
14	10	12	8	7	7	8	99
15	9	10	8	7	10	9	102

Figure 6.2: The Rainfall Spreadsheet

Position the cursor at A6 (which contains the label "HONOLU-LU") and enter the following sequence of commands:

/S#	{invoke the DIF storage command}
S	{to **save** a DIF file}
RAIN.DIF (return)	{enter the file name}
N15 (return)	{the lower-right position}
R	{to save the data by **rows**}

Notice we are calling this file RAIN.DIF.

For the purpose of examining a DIF file, we can write a simple BASIC program that will display the contents of such a file on the screen of your computer. In the next section of this chapter we will look at a display of RAIN.DIF. Then, in the following section we will study the BASIC program that created the display.

THE STRUCTURE OF DIF FILES

The display of the file RAIN.DIF appears in Figure 6.3. (Due to space constraints, the figure is arranged in arbitrary columns; but remember that the data represents one continuous file.) Take a brief look at it before we begin studying it in detail. You can easily spot all the data from the rainfall spreadsheet—first, the names of the cities, and then the rainfall values, taken from the columns of the original spreadsheet. But the rainfall values are interspersed with many other data items that do not make any immediate sense; these items are what we have described as the self-documentation feature of DIF files. They *describe* the contents of the file itself, and are designed for the convenience of the program that will read the file. As we study these items, a few of them may seem arbitrary and extraneous. This is partly because the DIF file format is designed to be flexible; some of the data items allow for eventual expanded uses of DIF. What you see in Figure 6.3 is the DIF format that *the VisiCalc program* can read and write. Other programs that also use DIF may have other requirements.

The DIF file consists of many short lines of text. Some lines contain two pieces of data (separated by commas), and others contain only one. We will see that many of the items in the file act as *markers*. Some markers divide up different sections of the file, and others serve as "flags" to indicate what kind of information is

```
TABLE
0,1
""
VECTORS
0,10
""
TUPLES
0,14
""
DATA
0,0
""
-1,0
BOT
1,0
"HONOLULU"
1,0
"LOS ANGL"
1,0
"SAN FRAN"
1,0
"DENVER"
1,0
"ST.LOUIS"
1,0
"NEW ORLN"
1,0
"CLEVELND"
1,0
"MIAMI"
1,0
"WASH DC"
1,0
"NEW YORK"
-1,0
BOT
0,11.18
V
0,7.62
V
0,11.18
V
0,1.52
V
0,4.83
V
0,11.43
V
0,6.6
V
0.5.59
V
0,6.6
V
0,6.86
V
-1,0
BOT
0,6.35
V
0,7.11
V
0,7.62
V
0,1.78
V
0,5.33
V
0,11.68
V
0,5.59
V
0,5.08
V
0,6.35
V
0,7.37
V
-1,0
BOT
0,8.13
V
0,5.59
V
0,6.35
V
0,3.05
V
0,7.62
V
0,13.97
V
0,7.87
V
0,5.33
V
0,8.38
V
0,9.4
V
-1,0
BOT
0,3.56
V
0,3.3
V
0,4.06
V
0,4.83
V
0,9.91
V
```

Figure 6.3: RAIN.DIF (continues)

```
0,10.67
V
0,8.89
V
0,9.3
V
0,7.37
V
0,8.38
V
-1,0
BOT
0,2.54
V
0,.25
V
0,1.02
V
0,6.86
V
0,9.91
V
0,10.67
V
0,8.89
V
0,15.49
V
0,9.55
V
0,8.89
V
-1,0
BOT
0,.76
V
0,0
V
0,.25
V
0,4.83
V
0,11.18
V
0,11.94
V
0,8.38
V
0,22.86
V
0,8.89
V
0,7.62
```

```
V
-1,0
BOT
0,1.52
V
0,0
V
0,0
V
0,4.57
V
0,9.4
V
0,17.02
V
0,3.89
V
0,17.53
V
0,10.41
V
0,9.4
V
-1,0
BOT
0,2.03
V
0,0
V
0,0
V
0,3.3
V
0,7.37
V
0,13.46
V
0,7.87
V
0,17.24
V
0,12.09
V
0,10.16
V
-1,0
BOT
0,1.78
V
0,.51
V
0,.51
V
```

Figure 6.3: RAIN.DIF (continues)

```
0,2.79                    0,6.86
V                         V
0,7.37                    0,7.37
V                         V
0,14.22                   0,9.65
V                         V
0,7.11                    -1,0
V                         BOT
0,22.1                    0,9.4
V                         V
0,7.87                    0,5.59
V                         V
0,8.38                    0,10.16
V                         V
-1,0                      0,1.02
BOT                       V
0,3.81                    0,5.08
V                         V
0,.76                     0,12.95
V                         V
0,2.54                    0,6.1
V                         V
0,2.79                    0,4.06
V                         V
0,7.11                    0,7.62
V                         V
0,5.84                    0,8.89
V                         V
0,6.6                     -1,0
V                         BOT
0,20.83                   0,58.68
V                         V
0,6.86                    0,35.81
V                         V
0,7.37                    0,49.53
V                         V
-1,0                      0,39.37
BOT                       V
0,7.62                    0,91.46
V                         V
0,5.08                    0,143.76
V                         V
0,5.84                    0,84.9
V                         V
0,2.03                    0,152.27
V                         V
0,6.35                    0,99.36
V                         V
0,9.91                    0,102.37
V                         V
0,7.11                    -1,0
V                         EOD
```

Figure 6.3: RAIN.DIF

coming up in the file. These markers are like the colored plastic dividers that you put in a looseleaf notebook. They allow you to see where one section ends and another begins, and they identify the contents of different sections.

Let's begin looking at the file in detail. The file is actually divided into two main parts. The first part, called the *header*, contains information about the way the data is organized. The second part, called the *data part*, stores the data itself.

The header of the file in Figure 6.3 consists of the first twelve lines of data:

```
TABLE
0,1
""
VECTORS
0,10
""
TUPLES
0,14
""
DATA
0,1
""
```

There are four different items in this header, each item containing three lines of data. The first line of each item is a descriptive title; the second line contains two numbers; and the third line is a *string* value. (A string is simply a nonnumeric value—another word for what VisiCalc calls a *label*.) Notice that all four of the strings in this header item are *empty strings*, represented by a pair of quotation marks with nothing between them.

We can look at this header section from two points of view. Remember that we will be writing one BASIC program that only needs to *read* a DIF file, and another that will have the task of *writing* a DIF file to return data to the VisiCalc program. From the point of view of a BASIC program that reads the file, there are exactly two relevant pieces of information in the header. (We will see in a moment which two items these are.) All the rest of the data can simply be read and forgotten. We will refer to this irrelevant data as "garbage." However, in order to read a DIF file successfully, the VisiCalc program *requires* this precise header format. What is garbage to one program is essential data to another. When we prepare the BASIC program that *writes* a DIF file to send data back to VisiCalc, we have to be careful to duplicate the entire DIF file in all its detail. Thus, while it is important to be able to recognize and duplicate the header section of the DIF file, only a limited part of the information it contains is actually relevant to the processing tasks we will perform in BASIC.

The two important pieces of information are contained in the header items titled VECTORS and TUPLES. These two items tell you exactly how many rows and columns of data have been taken from the VisiCalc spreadsheet to be stored in the DIF file. Don't be intimidated by the terms *vectors* and *tuples*; they are simply the DIF names for rows and columns.

The specific correspondence of rows and columns to vectors and tuples depends on how you originally store the DIF file when you use the VisiCalc /S# command. In the case of the rainfall spreadsheet, the file was stored by rows. The result is that the VECTORS header item tells how many rows there are, and the TUPLES item tells how many columns. The number appears as the second value of the second line of the header item. For example:

```
VECTORS
0,10
////
```

indicates that the file contains 10 vectors, and:

```
TUPLES
0,14
////
```

indicates 14 tuples.

Understanding the correspondence between VisiCalc rows and columns and DIF vectors and tuples can prove to be the most difficult part of reading the DIF file. The diagram in Figure 6.4 may clarify the situation for you.

The last header item is always the item titled DATA; it has an unchanging format:

```
DATA
0,0
////
```

This item is simply a marker for the end of the header section. In other words, it tells you that the data section is about to begin. It is a necessary item, because the header section is actually expandable. Other header items may appear between the TUPLES and DATA items for some DIF applications.

The second part of the DIF file—the data section—organizes the data from your VisiCalc spreadsheet by what DIF calls tuples. Each tuple is a section of data in the DIF file. All the tuples in a given file contain the same number of data items; these items are the vectors. As we have seen, tuples can store either rows or columns from your VisiCalc spreadsheet, depending on how you originally save the data. Look again at Figure 6.4. You can see that saving a DIF file by rows means that each DIF tuple will consist of a *column* of VisiCalc information. (Conversely, saving a DIF file by columns means that a tuple will contain a row of information.) Now look at the DIF file in Figure 6.3. The file was saved by rows, so the tuples contain columns of information. You can easily pick out the first tuple—it stores the first column of the spreadsheet, the names of the cities. The number of data items in each tuple is equal to the specified number of vectors in the DIF file.

The choice between storing a DIF file by rows or by columns from the /S# command, then, makes a significant difference in the

---

If you save the DIF file *by rows* from the VisiCalc /S# command:

    VECTORS
    0,⑩◄————*this value shows the number of rows.*
    ""

    TUPLES
    0,⑭◄————*this value shows the number of columns.*
    ""

If you save the DIF file *by columns* from the VisiCalc /S# command:

    VECTORS
    0,⑭◄————*this value shows the number of columns.*
    ""

    TUPLES
    0,⑩◄————*this value shows the number of rows.*
    ""

Figure 6.4: Rows and Columns; Vectors and Tuples

way the file is organized. This difference will be reflected in the way you write your BASIC program to read a DIF file for a given application.

The items of the data section are all presented in a two-line format. The first line contains two numbers (separated by a comma), and the second line consists of a string. The design of this format allows the data section to store different types of data and to specify clearly which type of data it *is* storing. There are actually three types of items in the data section of our DIF file: DIF markers, numeric data items, and string data items. The first number on the first line of each item is the *type indicator*; in our DIF file, this indicator is −1, 0, or 1. We will examine these three types one by one. Figure 6.5 gives an overview of the three types.

A DIF marker item in the data section is designated by a type indicator of −1. There is a marker at the beginning of each tuple in the data section. Here is what this marker looks like:

```
−1,0
BOT
```

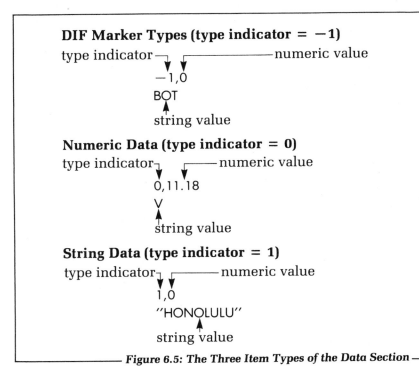

Figure 6.5: The Three Item Types of the Data Section

The value −1 indicates that this is a marker item. The letters BOT stand for "beginning of tuple." If you look down the DIF file in Figure 6.3, you will find that each tuple (i.e., each column of data from the VisiCalc spreadsheet) begins with one of these two-line markers. There is also a marker to designate the end of the file:

```
−1,0
EOD
```

The letters EOD stand for "end of data." Both the BOT and the EOD markers prove useful in certain programming situations, as we will see later on.

The other two types of items in the data section actually *contain* data—either labels or values—from the VisiCalc spreadsheet. The second type of item is the numeric data item. It is designated by a type indicator of 0. For example:

```
0,11.18
V
```

The 0 value would tell the program that reads the DIF file that this item contains a numeric value. The data value itself is found directly after the type indicator, on the same line—11.18, in this particular item. The "V" in the second line stands for value. It simply indicates that the number 11.18 is in fact a valid numeric value. The DIF file can also store NA and ERROR values from the VisiCalc spreadsheet. These would appear as follows:

```
0,0
ERROR

0,0
NA
```

The third and final type of item in the data section is the string data item. It contains an item indicator of 1. For example:

```
1,0
"HONOLULU"
```

Notice that the string value itself, in the second line of the item, is contained within quotation marks. This punctuation is actually optional in the DIF format, but it is there for the benefit of certain versions of the BASIC language that require the quotation marks in order to read some strings.

At this point you may be asking yourself what the rationale is for this two-line, three-type system of data item representation.

Very simply, it is designed to give clear guidelines to any program that is reading the DIF file. Just like the label on a can of soup, which tells you what kind of soup you can expect to find inside, the type indicator tells the reading program what *type* of data it will find stored in the data item. This is a significant issue. Programming languages like BASIC handle the storage of strings and numerical values in different ways. When you write input statements in a BASIC program, you have to specify what type of data the program should expect to read—numerical or nonnumerical. You can design a BASIC program to test the value of the DIF data type indicator as a first step in the process of reading data from a DIF file. If the type indicator is 1, as in the following sequence:

        1,0

        "HELLO"

then the program can treat the 0 as garbage, and store the string "HELLO" as the relevant part of this data item. On the other hand, if the type indicator is 0, as follows:

        0,100

        V

then the program knows that it is to read and store the numeric value, 100, and treat the "V" as garbage.

In summary, we have seen that the DIF file supplies, in addition to the actual data it is storing, a lot of important information about itself:

- The header section of the DIF file indicates how much data is stored in the file, and how the data is organized. This information is expressed in terms of VECTORS and TUPLES. The correspondence between vectors, tuples, rows, and columns depends on how the DIF file was saved.
- The data section of the DIF file has *markers* that indicate the beginning of the tuples (BOT) and the end of the file (EOD).
- Each data item has a systematic method of indicating what *type* of data it contains.

All this information is designed to aid the program that is reading the DIF file. You may have realized by now that some of the information is actually redundant. For example, if you know how many tuples the file contains, and how many data values are in each tuple (i.e., the number of vectors), then you don't really need the BOT markers. You can determine the beginning of each tuple by counting data items.

However, this redundancy is a deliberate part of the DIF design. Different applications may make use of different DIF features. Each application will use the features that are most convenient for the task at hand.

Our first BASIC program is a very simple one, but it will nonetheless illustrate how some of the DIF features facilitate file reading in BASIC.

A BASIC PROGRAM FOR DISPLAYING DIF FILES

The DIF file display program, shown in Figure 6.6, is the first of three BASIC programs we will examine in the final chapters of this book. Even if you have little or no experience with BASIC programming, you should be able to *use* these programs on your personal computer. In addition to the brief summary of BASIC in Appendix B, the Bibliography refers to several books on BASIC programming and on data file programming that will also be helpful. Certain parts of these programs—specifically, the file handling subroutines—will need to be revised for different versions of BASIC. Appendix A provides these subroutines for the BASICs of three popular personal computers. We will discuss how to use these subroutines in the next section of this chapter.

When you run this first program, the following messages will appear on the screen:

```
DISPLAY A DIF FILE
= = = = = = =   =   = = =   = = = =

NAME OF FILE? □
```

At this point the program waits for you to type the name of the DIF file that you want to examine. Make sure you have the correct data disk in your disk drive before you enter the file name. Once you specify a file name, the screen will clear and the DIF file will be listed, line by line, on the screen.

Let's briefly examine the structure of this program. The first 13 lines (i.e., lines 10 to 130) make up the "main program" section. This section merely reads the name of the file that you want to display, and then calls the subroutines that do the work of opening, reading, and closing the file. (A *subroutine* in BASIC is a group of isolated lines that are devoted to a certain task. You "call" a subroutine with the GOSUB statement. At the end of each subroutine, a RETURN statement sends control of the program back to the line following the original GOSUB statement.)

Line 40 of the main program section clears the screen with the instruction:

HOME

The screen goes blank, and the cursor moves to the upper-left corner. Some versions of BASIC use the command:

CLS

```
10 REM *** THIS PROGRAM DISPLAYS
20 REM *** A DIF FILE
30 REM *** ON YOUR SCREEN.
40 HOME : REM "CLS" IN SOME BASICS.
50 PRINT "DISPLAY A DIF FILE"
60 PRINT "======= = === ===="
70 PRINT : PRINT : PRINT
80 INPUT "NAME OF FILE? "; F$
90 HOME
100 GOSUB 1000 : REM OPEN FILE FOR READING
110 GOSUB 200  : REM READ AND DISPLAY FILE
120 GOSUB 1200 : REM CLOSE FILE
130 END
200 REM *** READ AND DISPLAY FILE
210 Q$ = CHR$(34) : REM QUOTATION MARK
220 GOSUB 2000 : REM READ HEADER ITEM
230 PRINT T$
240 PRINT V1;",";V2
250 PRINT Q$; S$; Q$
260 IF T$ <> "DATA" GOTO 220
270 GOSUB 2100 : REM READ DATA ITEM
280 PRINT V1;",";V2
290 IF V1 = 1 THEN PRINT Q$;S$;Q$
300 IF V1 <> 1 THEN PRINT S$
310 IF S$ <> "EOD" GOTO 270
320 RETURN
1000 REM *** OPEN FILE FOR READING
        **** see Appendix A ****
1200 REM *** CLOSE FILE
        **** see Appendix A ****
2000 REM *** READ HEADER ITEM
        **** see Appendix A ****
2100 REM *** READ DATA ITEM
        **** see Appendix A ****
```

Figure 6.6: First BASIC Program: Displaying a DIF File

rather than HOME, so you may have to revise this particular line. Lines 50 and 60 print the title of the program, and line 70 skips three lines by executing the PRINT instruction three times:

```
70 PRINT : PRINT : PRINT
```

Line 80 is the INPUT statement for the file name:

```
80 INPUT "NAME OF FILE? ";F$
```

In some versions of BASIC, the INPUT statement automatically supplies a question mark after an input prompt. If your BASIC does this, then you should revise line 80 as follows:

```
80 INPUT "NAME OF FILE";F$
```

Lines 100, 110, and 120 are the subroutine calls:

```
100 GOSUB 1000
110 GOSUB 200
120 GOSUB 1200
```

The subroutine at line 1000 opens a disk file for reading. The real workhorse subroutine of this program is at line 200; it actually reads the DIF file and displays it on the screen. The subroutine at line 1200 closes the file. We will discuss the file-handling subroutines in the next section of this chapter.

The subroutine at line 200 calls two further subroutines on its own—one designed to read a header item, and another to read a data item. These subroutines (at lines 2000 and 2100, respectively) read the lines of the file and assign the values to certain variables. The subroutine at line 200 then uses these variables to display the data. Let's see exactly how this works.

The header-reading subroutine (at line 2000) assigns the header-item title to the variable T$; the numerical values to the variables V1 and V2; and the string value to S$. Lines 220 to 250, then, print a single header item on the screen:

```
220 GOSUB 2000
230 PRINT T$
240 PRINT V1;",",";V2
250 PRINT Q$;S$;Q$
```

The variable Q$ contains the quotation mark character, which is 34 on the ASCII character code:

```
210 Q$ = CHR$(34)
```

This variable is used to simulate the exact contents of the string items in the file.

Line 260 repeatedly loops back to line 220 to display another header item, until the DATA item—the final item of the header section—has been read and displayed:

```
260 IF T$ <> "DATA" GOTO 220
```

This is the first example of the use of a DIF file marker to guide the action of the program.

Lines 270 to 310 print the data section of the program. The subroutine at line 2100 assigns the numerical values to V1 and V2, and the string value to S$; line 280 prints the numerical values with a comma between them:

```
270 GOSUB 2100
280 PRINT V1;",";V2
```

If the string value is actually a label from the VisiCalc spreadsheet, then it must be displayed with quotation marks around it. If it is a DIF marker (BOT, EOD, or V) then it should appear without quotes. Lines 290 and 300 make use of the type indicator, stored in variable V1, to decide how to display the string value:

```
290 IF V1 = 1 THEN PRINT Q$;S$;Q$
300 IF V1 <> 1 THEN PRINT S$
```

Finally, line 310 sends control of the program back up to line 270 repeatedly until the EOD marker—the last item of the file—has been read:

```
310 IF S$ <> "EOD" GOTO 270
```

When the whole file has been displayed, line 320 returns control back to the main program section:

```
320 RETURN
```

The main weakness of this program is that it never stops to let you view the DIF file data at your leisure. The data scrolls in and out of view rather quickly, which can be inconvenient if you need to examine one particular part of the data. There are several ways to remedy this, depending on your computer and your needs. Most obviously, you can *print* the file data on paper rather than just displaying it on the screen. Alternatively, you might be able to stop the action of the program temporarily by typing a special control character offered for that purpose by some computer systems. Finally, if neither of these solutions is satisfactory, you may be able to add a subroutine to your program that will stop the action and wait for you to input a command to continue. This routine might look something like this:

```
400 INPUT "PRESS <RETURN> TO CONTINUE. ";A$
410 RETURN
```

You can call this routine at intervals during the display of the file. Note that this routine is only possible if your version of BASIC lets you input data from the keyboard while an external data file is open for reading.

We will be using the four file-handling subroutines of this program (at lines 1000, 1200, 2000, and 2100) again in the BASIC programs of Chapters 7 and 8. In addition, we'll need several other file-handling subroutines. All together, they will form a small "library" of reusable routines devoted to input and output of DIF file data. In the next section we will discuss the use of these routines.

THE FILE-HANDLING SUBROUTINES

All eight of the file-handling subroutines in this library are very short. Unfortunately, the BASIC instructions that open, close, read, and write external files vary significantly from one version of BASIC to another. The *concepts* of file handling are the same, but the syntax of the commands used to carry out the actions changes.

For this reason, it always makes sense to isolate all the file-handling instructions in easily identified, and easily revised routines of their own. That is exactly what we will do in the three BASIC programs of this book. Most of the remaining sections of the programs should work, with very little revision, on almost any BASIC. But the file routines must be tailored specifically to the computer you are working with.

The eight file routines that you will need for these programs are identified and described in Figure 6.7. For the actual lines of BASIC code that you will type into your computer, you'll have to refer to Appendix A, which supplies three different versions of these routines. If you are using one of the three computers mentioned, you should have no problem including the subroutines in

Line Number of Subroutine	Description
1000	Opens a file for *reading* data. File name must be assigned to F$ before you call this subroutine.
1100	Opens a file for *writing* data. File name must be assigned to F$ before you call this subroutine.
1200	Closes a file.
2000	Reads a header item. Returns values as follows: T$ = title V1 = first numeric value V2 = second numeric value S$ = string value
2100	Reads a data item. Returns values as follows: V1 = type indicator V2 = numeric value S$ = string value
3000	Writes a header item. In advance of calling this routine, you must assign values as follows: T$ = title V1 = first value V2 = second value S$ = string value
3100	Writes a data item *without* quotes around the string. In advance of calling this routine, you must assign values as follows: V1 = type indicator V2 = numeric value S$ = string value
3200	Writes a data item *with* quotes around the string. In advance of calling this routine, you must assign values as follows: V1 = type indicator V2 = numeric value S$ = string value

Figure 6.7: The File-Handling Subroutines

with the rest of the program. If you are using another computer, you will have to do some research into how your version of BASIC performs file-handling functions. The chances are good that your BASIC will be similar to one of the three listed in Appendix A.

Notice the difference between the routines that read data and the routines that write data. After calling the read-data routines, the data that has been read is available in the specified variables. *Before* you call the write-data routines, however, you must *assign* values to the specified variables. All variables are *global* in BASIC; that is to say, a value assigned to a variable in one routine is available to all routines of the program.

SUMMARY

DIF files can be created or read by the VisiCalc program. They are valuable for exchanging data both between different spreadsheets and between BASIC programs and VisiCalc spreadsheets.

The structure of DIF files is designed to make the inner organization of the data storage evident to the program that reads the file. For this reason, VisiCalc DIF files actually contain two kinds of information—self-documentation, and the spreadsheet data itself. All this information is divided into two sections in the DIF file—the header and the data section. The header tells how many data items the file contains, and, indirectly, the number of spreadsheet rows and columns it copied the items from. The data section has an elegant system for indicating what *type* of data is contained in each item. This is essential for efficient reading of the data by BASIC programs.

We have seen a simple BASIC program that reads and displays, but does *not* store, the data from a DIF file. The tasks of storing and using DIF file data are somewhat more complicated, as we will see in the next chapter.

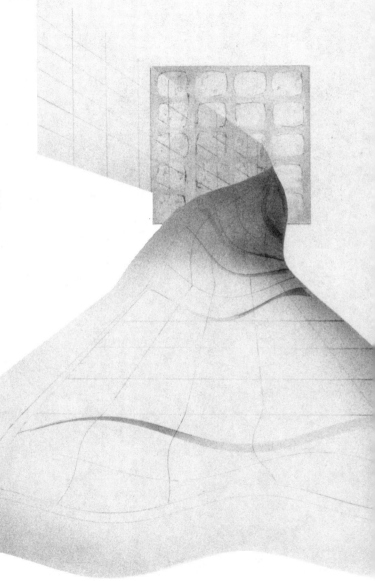

CHAPTER SEVEN

DIF FILES, PART II: READING A DIF FILE FROM BASIC

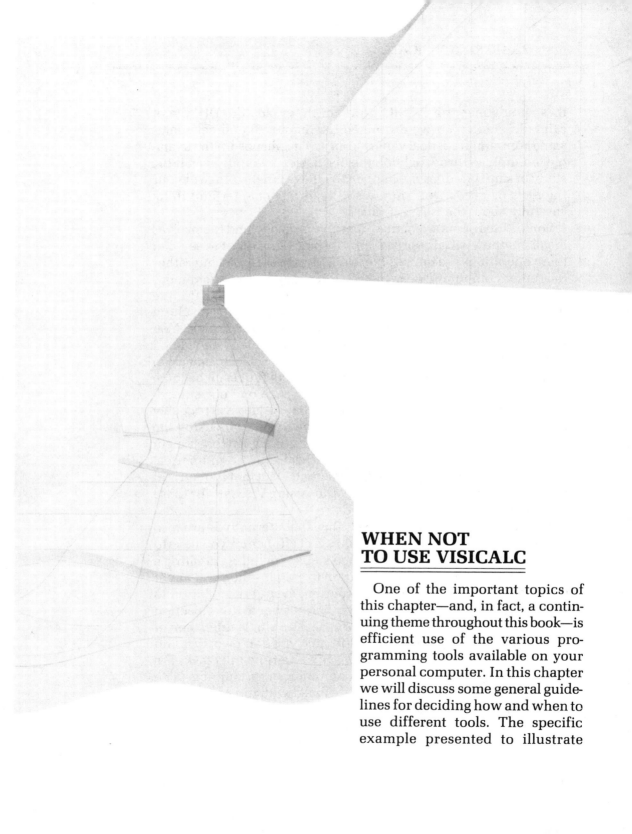

WHEN NOT
TO USE VISICALC

One of the important topics of this chapter—and, in fact, a continuing theme throughout this book—is efficient use of the various programming tools available on your personal computer. In this chapter we will discuss some general guidelines for deciding how and when to use different tools. The specific example presented to illustrate these guidelines is a BASIC program that reads the DIF file of rainfall data (which we examined in Chapter 6) and calculates some common statistical values from it. The purpose of the example is simply to throw light on the discussion at hand. Even if the study of statistics does not happen to fall within the range of your interests or needs, you should still read this chapter and think carefully about the issues it raises.

Some kinds of mathematical operations do not lend themselves ideally to the VisiCalc spreadsheet format. This is not to say that these operations are impossible to perform in VisiCalc, but rather that other computer programming tools may handle them more efficiently. In general, whenever a calculation involves finding many *intermediate* values on the way to an eventual resulting value, that calculation may be somewhat clumsy in VisiCalc. You may find yourself filling up a spreadsheet with many calculated values that you have no real interest in. Once the major calculation is complete, the intermediate values that led to the result become irrelevant—but there they are, taking up space on your spreadsheet. What is worse is that these intermediate values will probably take you an unreasonable amount of time to compute using the VisiCalc program. Remember that VisiCalc is designed for efficient calculation *and presentation* of numerical and nonnumerical data. If you are creating lots of intermediate data that is of no real use to you, then you may be wasting time using VisiCalc for those particular calculations.

You may be thinking, however, that the alternatives are also very time-consuming. If, in the interests of efficiency, you have to go through a number of complicated steps—including creating a DIF file and writing a BASIC program to read it—then you might prefer to stay with the VisiCalc program, even if the solution to your task proves to be a little clumsy. The answer to this objection is simple. If you only have to perform a task a single time, then of course you do it as quickly as possible, and you don't worry much about the elegance of your solution. But one-time-only tasks are rare in life, and even rarer in computer programming. The chances are good that the job you are faced with today will come up again tomorrow or next week or next month. The time you spend today developing the best solution for the job will be more than compensated when you have to perform the same job in the future.

Furthermore, the difficulty of writing BASIC programs to deal with DIF files decreases each time you write a new one. The key to this decreasing difficulty is the use of subroutines. We have already built a small library of short, very low-level subroutines that take care of the mechanics of opening, reading, and writing files. In this chapter we will expand that library with three higher-level subroutines that we will be able to use again in the program of Chapter 8.

In addition, as you become familiar with the world of BASIC programming, you will find many sources of subroutines for almost any programming task you can imagine. In the end, if you plan carefully, you will discover that writing a program in BASIC consists mostly of gathering up the needed subroutines—from your own library, or from other sources you have access to—and piecing them together to solve your specific problem.

The rainfall spreadsheet is a typical example of a situation where you might wisely choose to team the VisiCalc program with a BASIC program of your own design to meet all your data processing needs. Let's review the steps we will follow to make this combination a viable one:

- Use the VisiCalc program for inputting the raw data. We have already seen that VisiCalc is clearly ideal for this task. When you have entered all the data required for a given application onto your spreadsheet, you can take as much time as necessary to check it over and verify its accuracy. If any value is incorrect, you can easily re-enter it without affecting the rest of the data.

- When the input and verification step is complete, create a DIF file of the raw data. Using the VisiCalc /S# command, this step takes only a few seconds.

- Read the DIF file from a BASIC program. (By the end of this chapter, you will be familiar with a complete set of subroutines for reading DIF file data and storing it in a BASIC *array* structure.)

- Use a short and simple BASIC routine to perform the statistical calculations and display the results on the screen.

In summary, here are four questions you can ask yourself about any data processing job you are considering for the VisiCalc program:

1. Does the task involve a large amount of raw data that must be input accurately and reliably?

2. Do the subsequent calculations on this data require formulas or intermediate values that would be difficult, clumsy, or inefficient to produce with VisiCalc?

3. Is this a job you are likely to have to perform more than once?

4. Can you easily write—or find—the appropriate BASIC subroutines to perform the problematic calculations?

If you find yourself answering "yes" to these questions, then your task is probably an ideal candidate for the *combined* powers of the VisiCalc program and BASIC.

STATISTICS FROM THE RAINFALL SPREADSHEET

The statistical values that we will calculate for each city of the rainfall spreadsheet are the *variance* and the *standard deviation*. These are both measurements of dispersion from the mean. In other words, they describe how a series of data varies from the average value of the series.

You can calculate the variance and the standard deviation as follows:

1. Compute the mean (average) value of the series.

2. Subtract each value from the mean value, and square the difference.

3. Find the sum of all the difference-squared values from step 2.

4. Divide the sum (from step 3) by the number of values minus 1; this value is the variance.

5. Take the square root of the variance; this value is the standard deviation.

If you were to perform these steps on a VisiCalc spreadsheet, the intermediate values from step 2 would create as large a table of numbers as the original rainfall data. In BASIC, however, these intermediate values do not need to be stored; rather as each value is calculated, it can be added on to a running total.

Figure 7.1 shows the output from the BASIC program that we will be examining in this chapter. The program is easy to use. It begins by displaying a title at the top of the screen:

```
STATISTICS   FROM   A   DIF   FILE
= = = = = = = = = =   = = = =   =   = = =   = = = =
```

and then prompts you to enter the name of the DIF file that you want to work with:

```
NAME OF FILE?
```

At this point, make sure you have the correct data disk in your disk drive, and enter the file name RAIN.DIF. The disk drive will then activate, and the message:

```
READING FILE.
```

will appear on the screen. After a few seconds of reading and calculation, the program will display a three-column table on the screen. The first column will contain the names of the cities; the

```
STATISTICS FROM A DIF FILE
========== ==== = === ====


NAME OF FILE? RAIN.DIF


READING FILE.

CITY            VAR.            ST.DEV.
====            ====            =======
HONOLULU        12.25           3.5
LOS ANGL        9.26            3.04
SAN FRAN        16.42           4.05
DENVER          2.89            1.7
ST.LOUIS        4.35            2.08
NEW ORLN        7.57            2.75
CLEVELND        2.12            1.46
MIAMI           53.88           7.34
WASH DC         2.9             1.7
NEW YORK        1.09            1.05
```

Figure 7.1: Output from the DIF Statistics Program

second, the variances; and the third, the standard deviations of the rainfall data.

STORING A DIF FILE IN BASIC

The listing of the DIF statistics program appears in Figure 7.2. The three subroutines at lines 300, 400, and 500 are responsible for reading the DIF file and storing the spreadsheet data in two BASIC *arrays*. These three subroutines will appear again in the sort program of Chapter 8. We will look at them first, then we will study the statistics subroutine.

An array is a *data structure* that stores tables of numerical or nonnumerical values. All the data in a given BASIC array must be of the same type, but we may define both numerical arrays and string arrays for use in a BASIC program. Clearly an array is an ideal structure for storing spreadsheet data from a DIF file. We will actually define two arrays in this program, a two-dimensional array to store the rows and columns of numbers, and a one-dimensional string array to store the names of the cities.

A BASIC array is defined in a DIM statement. Line 90 defines the two arrays used in this program:

```
90 DIM T1(T,V), T1$(V)
```

The name of the two-dimensional numerical array is T1; it is defined to store up to T columns and V rows of data. The string array, T1$, will hold up to V string values. Since the variables T and V are used in the definition of arrays T1 and T1$, we clearly must assign values to T and V before coming to the DIM statement. Where do you suppose these two values will come from? Of course, from the header section of the DIF file.

Take a look at the subroutine that begins at line 300 of the program. This subroutine controls the reading of the header, and gleans from it the two relevant pieces of information—the number of rows and the number of columns contained in the spreadsheet data. You'll recall that the subroutine at line 2000 reads one three-line header item:

```
310 GOSUB 2000
```

The title of the item is read into T$, and the value that we're interested in is read into V2. As each header item is read, the program

```
10 REM *** STATISTICAL PACKAGE FOR DIF
20 HOME : REM ** "CLS" FOR SOME BASICS
30 PRINT "STATISTICS FROM A DIF FILE"
40 PRINT "========== ==== = === ===="
50 PRINT : PRINT : PRINT
60 INPUT "NAME OF FILE? "; F$
65 PRINT
70 GOSUB 1000 : REM ** OPEN FILE
80 GOSUB 300 : REM ** READ HEADER
90 DIM T1(T,V), T1$(V)
95 PRINT : PRINT "READING FILE." : PRINT
100 GOSUB 400 : REM ** READ STRINGS
110 GOSUB 500 : REM ** READ NUMBERS
115 GOSUB 1200 : REM ** CLOSE FILE
120 PRINT "CITY", "VAR.", "ST.DEV"
130 PRINT "====", "====", "======"
135 DEF FNR(X) = INT(100 * X + .5)/100
140 FOR I = 1 TO V
145    PRINT T1$(I),
150    GOSUB 3500 : REM ** STATISTICS SUBROUTINE
160 NEXT I
170 END

300 REM *** READ HEADER
310 GOSUB 2000
320 IF T$ = "VECTORS" THEN V = V2
330 IF T$ = "TUPLES" THEN T = V2 - 1
340 IF T$ <> "DATA" THEN GOTO 310
350 RETURN

400 REM *** READ STRINGS
410 GOSUB 2100 : REM ** GARBAGE
420 FOR I = 1 TO V
430    GOSUB 2100 : REM ** READ DATA ITEM
440    T1$(I) = S$
450 NEXT I
460 RETURN

500 REM *** READ NUMBERS
510 FOR I = 1 TO T
520    GOSUB 2100 : REM ** BOT -- GARBAGE
530    FOR J = 1 TO V
540      GOSUB 2100
550      T1(I,J) = V2
560    NEXT J
570 NEXT I
580 RETURN

1000 REM *** OPEN FILE FOR READING
        *** SEE APPENDIX A ***

1200 REM *** CLOSE FILE
        *** SEE APPENDIX A ***

2000 REM *** READ HEADER ITEM
        *** SEE APPENDIX A ***

2100 REM *** READ DATA ITEM
        *** SEE APPENDIX A ***
```

Figure 7.2: The DIF Statistics Program (continues)

```
3500 REM *** STATISTICS
3510 T3 = 0
3520 FOR J = 1 TO T - 1
3530    T3 = T3 + T1(J,I)
3540 NEXT J
3550 M3 = T3/(T - 1)
3560 V3 = 0
3570 FOR J = 1 TO T - 1
3580    V3 = V3 + (M3 - T1(J,I))^2
3590 NEXT J
3600 V3 = V3/(T - 2)
3610 S3 = SQR(V3)
3620 PRINT FNR(V3), FNR(S3)
3630 RETURN
```

Figure 7.2: The DIF Statistics Program

checks T\$ to see if it is either the VECTORS item or the TUPLES item. If the item is either one of these, then the appropriate variable (T or V) is assigned a value from V2:

320 IF T\$ = "VECTORS" THEN V = V2
330 IF T\$ = "TUPLES" THEN T = V2 − 1

Then the subroutine repeatedly loops back to read another header item, until the DATA item is read:

340 IF T\$ <> "DATA" THEN GOTO 310

From this subroutine alone, you begin to see that this program makes certain assumptions about the DIF file—and indirectly, about the VisiCalc spreadsheet—it is reading. The assumptions are as follows:

1. The first column of the spreadsheet must be a column of labels.

2. The last column of the spreadsheet must represent the sums (across the rows) of the rest of the spreadsheet data.

3. The DIF file must be stored by rows (from the /S# command) so that each tuple represents a column of data. The first tuple, then, will contain string values, and the last will contain the row-totals.

If you should, by mistake, direct the program to read a DIF file that does not meet these specifications, the results will be unpredictable. In this sense, this program is designed for a specific kind of spreadsheet. However, the program is also flexible in one essential aspect: the spreadsheet can contain an unlimited number of rows and columns. Thus, if the rainfall spreadsheet grows to include more cities, this program—and the sort program in Chapter 8—will both continue to function correctly.

The subroutine at line 300 is called from the main program, just before the DIM statement:

```
80 GOSUB 300
90 DIM T1(T,V), T1$(V)
```

Thanks to the VECTORS and TUPLES items in the header, then, the values V and T can be used to define the two arrays to the exact length necessary to store all the spreadsheet data.

Once these two arrays have been defined, the program can begin assigning them values from the DIF file. The subroutine at line 400 reads the string values from the first tuple, and assigns them to the array T1$. The subroutine at line 500 reads the numeric values from the remaining tuples, and assigns them to the array T1. Both of these subroutines are called from the main program section, just after the DIM statement:

```
100 GOSUB 400
110 GOSUB 500
```

The subroutine at line 400 begins by reading the BOT marker as garbage:

```
410 GOSUB 2100
```

What this means, exactly, is that the file item has been read, but the program will make no use of the values it contains. Next, within a FOR loop, each of the string values is read and stored in the array T1$. The values T (the number of tuples/columns) and V (the number of vectors/rows) continue to control the action of the program. For example, thanks to the value V, the subroutine at line 400 knows exactly how many string values to read. These string values are returned in the variable S$ from the subroutine at line 2100:

```
420 FOR I = 1 TO V
430     GOSUB 2100
440     T1$(I) = S$
450 NEXT I
```

The subroutine at line 500 requires a pair of *nested* FOR loops (i.e., a loop within a loop) to read the tuples of numeric data. The outer loop reads each tuple, one by one:

```
510 FOR I = 1 TO T
```

and the inner loop reads each value of a given tuple:

```
530 FOR J = 1 TO V
```

The value of T is actually one less than the total number of tuples in the DIF file. (Look back at line 330 to see that this is true.) This is because the first tuple contains strings, not numbers.

The first item read in each tuple is garbage—the BOT marker:

```
520 GOSUB 2100
```

Subsequently, within the inner loop, the returned value of the numerical data—in the variable V2—is assigned to the array T1:

```
540 GOSUB 2100
550 T1(I,J) = V2
```

Within the context of the kind of spreadsheet we have specified (i.e., containing a first column of strings, and a final column of totals; saved by rows as a DIF file), these three subroutines—at lines 300, 400, and 500—are flexible and reliable for reading the data and storing it in arrays.

THE STATISTICS SUBROUTINE

The subroutine that calculates the variance and the standard deviation from each city's rainfall data begins at line 3500. The main program section calls it once for each city—within a FOR loop:

```
140 FOR I = 1 TO V
145    PRINT T1$(I),
150    GOSUB 3500
160 NEXT I
```

Notice that this loop begins by printing the name of the city; the statistics subroutine then prints the two statistical values.

It only takes a dozen or so lines of BASIC code to calculate and print the variance and the standard deviation. For each city, the statistics subroutine takes one value from each tuple to carry out its calculations. (Each tuple, that is, except the last one, which contains the column of totals. This column of data is not used in the statistics program.) The first five executable lines of the subroutine calculate the average value from a given city's rainfall data. This value is assigned to the variable M3:

```
3510 T3 = 0
3520 FOR J = 1 TO T − 1
3530    T3 = T3 + T1(J,I)
3540 NEXT J
3550 M3 = T3/(T − 1)
```

Then a second FOR loop sums up the squares of the differences between the mean and the monthly values:

```
3560 V3 = 0
3570 FOR J = 1 TO T − 1
3580    V3 = V3 + (M3 − T1(J,I))^2
3590 NEXT J
```

Notice that the intermediate values—$(M3 − T1(J,I))^2$—are not saved but simply added on to the running total accumulating in the variable V3. Finally, the variance (V3) and the standard deviation (S3) are computed:

```
3600 V3 = V3/(T − 2)
3610 S3 = SQR(V3)
```

Before these values are printed, they are rounded off to the nearest hundredth by the user-defined function, FNR:

```
3620 PRINT FNR(V3), FNR(S3)
```

This function is defined in the main program section, at line 135:

```
135 DEF FNR(X) = INT(100 * X + .5)/100
```

You might recognize this as being very similar to the rounding function that we developed for a VisiCalc spreadsheet back in Chapter 3. VisiCalc and BASIC may appear to operate in very different ways, but they actually have many similar features.

SUMMARY

Sometimes you may encounter large data processing tasks in which the mathematical formulas are too complex to be handled conveniently by the VisiCalc program. In such cases it is sensible to consider using VisiCalc only for the data entry, and then transferring the data to a BASIC program via a DIF file. There are several factors to consider when you are deciding whether or not it is worth the trouble to write a BASIC program for processing VisiCalc data. Two of these factors are: the number of times you expect to have to use the program; and the difficulty of writing (or finding) the necessary BASIC subroutines to build the program. In the end, personal preference may also play a large part in the decision.

We have looked at a program that applies some statistical calculations to the values of a DIF file. The reusable subroutines of this program—which we will add to our "library" of DIF file subroutines—are the three that read the DIF file data and assign it to two BASIC arrays. These arrays correspond remarkably well to the structure of the VisiCalc spreadsheet. The three subroutines expect a spreadsheet with a first column of strings and a last column of totals. The resulting DIF file must be saved by rows. However, the subroutines do not specify a limit on the number of rows or columns of the spreadsheet.

In Chapter 8 we will go one step further in BASIC programming for DIF files. We will learn to write a new DIF file to return data to the VisiCalc program.

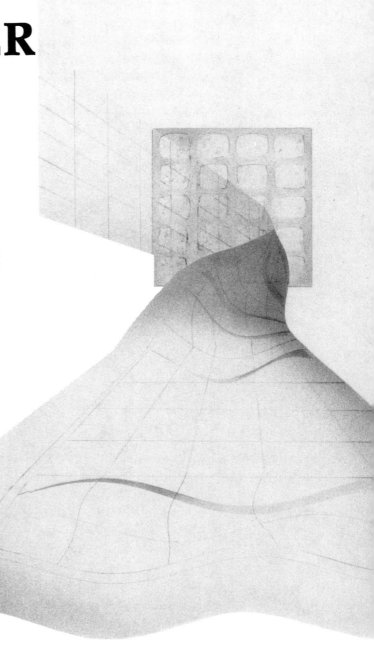

CHAPTER EIGHT

DIF FILES, PART III: WRITING A DIF FILE FROM BASIC

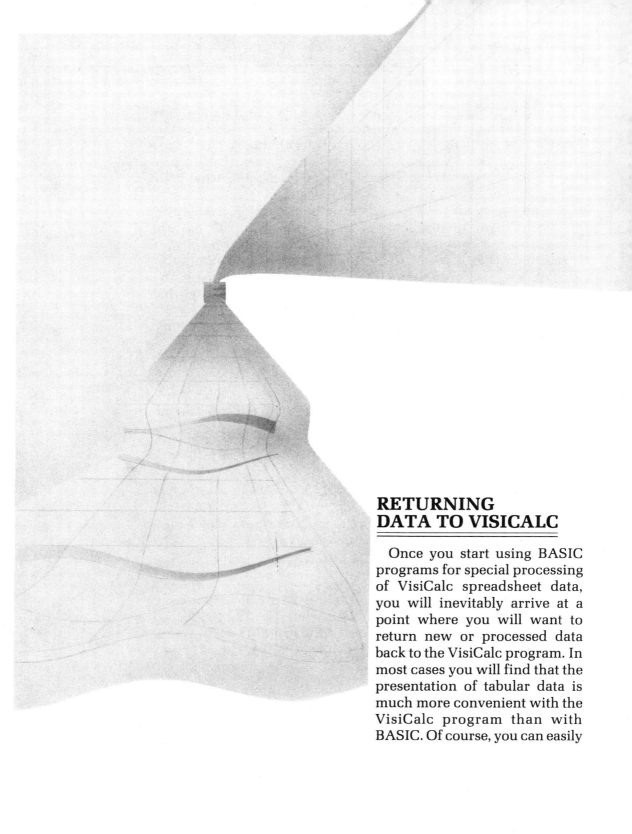

RETURNING
DATA TO VISICALC

Once you start using BASIC
programs for special processing
of VisiCalc spreadsheet data,
you will inevitably arrive at a
point where you will want to
return new or processed data
back to the VisiCalc program. In
most cases you will find that the
presentation of tabular data is
much more convenient with the
VisiCalc program than with
BASIC. Of course, you can easily

write a BASIC subroutine to present a small table of numbers, as we did in the statistics program of Chapter 7; however, once this table appears on the screen, it is completely static. To change the table in any way, you have to revise and re-run the BASIC program that created the table. In the VisiCalc program, on the other hand, you can reformat data, add rows and columns, change parameter values, and make any number of other revisions instantly.

So, for many applications it makes sense to add another step to the process of teaming up BASIC and VisiCalc—the capacity for returning DIF files to VisiCalc from a BASIC program. In this chapter we will look at an example of the completed process. The example, a sort program, may well prove to be a valuable tool that you'll use often for many different spreadsheet applications. Sorting is a task that is definitely not practical in VisiCalc, but quite simple in BASIC.

The sorting process illustrated in this chapter requires that you follow a specific sequence of steps:

1. Enter the raw data onto a VisiCalc spreadsheet. Include a column of labels on the left and a column of totals on the right of the spreadsheet.

2. Save the data in a DIF file, using the /S# command. Save the file by rows.

3. Run the BASIC sort program. (We will see how to do this in the next section of this chapter.) The sort program will create a new DIF file, containing the original data sorted either alphabetically or numerically.

4. Return to VisiCalc, and load the sorted DIF file onto the spreadsheet.

We will see that writing a DIF file from BASIC is scarcely harder than reading one. The same understanding of the DIF format is required, along with a new set of file-handling subroutines. Once these subroutines are written, however, they can be reused for many different applications.

A SORTING PROGRAM FOR DIF FILES

The complete dialogue produced by the sort program is shown in Figure 8.1. The listing of the program appears in Figure 8.2.

The program begins by displaying a title, and then prompts you to enter the name of the DIF file that you want to sort:

```
SORT  A  DIF  FILE
====  =  ===  ====
```

NAME OF FILE?

At this point you must make sure that the correct data disk is in your disk drive; when you are ready, you can enter the name of the file that you want to sort. In the sample dialogue the file name used is RAIN.DIF.

The sort program does not output any data to the screen. The real output from the program is a new DIF file, stored on your disk. However, the program displays several messages on the screen telling you what it is doing during run time. The first message is:

READING FILE.

When you see this message, you know that the program has found RAIN.DIF on the disk, and is reading it and storing its data in the

```
SORT A DIF FILE
==== = === ====


NAME OF FILE? RAIN.DIF


READING FILE.

A(LPHA OR N(UMERIC SORT? A

SORTING FILE.

WRITING FILE.

*******************

FILE ARAIN.DIF SAVED.
```

Figure 8.1: Dialogue from the DIF File Sorting Program

```
10 REM *** PROGRAM TO SORT A DIF FILE
20 HOME : REM ** "CLS" IN SOME BASICS
30 PRINT "SORT A DIF FILE"
40 PRINT "==== = === ===="
50 PRINT : PRINT : PRINT
60 INPUT "NAME OF FILE? "; F$
70 PRINT : PRINT
80 GOSUB 1000 : REM ** OPEN FILE FOR READING
90 GOSUB 300 : REM ** READ HEADER
100 DIM T1(T,V), T1$(V)
105 PRINT : PRINT "READING FILE." : PRINT
110 GOSUB 400 : REM ** READ STRINGS
120 GOSUB 500 : REM ** READ NUMBERS
130 GOSUB 1200 : REM ** CLOSE FILE
140 INPUT "A(LPHA OR N(UMERIC SORT? "; A$
150 IF A$ <> "A" AND A$ <> "N" THEN 140
160 F$ = A$ + F$
170 PRINT : PRINT "SORTING FILE."
180 GOSUB 4000 : REM ** SORT FILE
190 PRINT : PRINT "WRITING FILE."
200 GOSUB 1100 : REM ** OPEN FOR WRITING
210 GOSUB 600 : REM ** CREATE NEW FILE
220 GOSUB 1200 : REM ** CLOSE FILE
230 PRINT : PRINT "********************"
240 PRINT : PRINT "FILE "; F$; " SAVED."
250 END

300 REM *** READ HEADER
310 GOSUB 2000
320 IF T$ = "VECTORS" THEN V = V2
330 IF T$ = "TUPLES" THEN T = V2 - 1
340 IF T$ <> "DATA" THEN 310
350 RETURN

400 REM *** READ STRINGS
410 GOSUB 2100 : REM ** BOT --- GARBAGE
420 FOR I = 1 TO V
430   GOSUB 2100 : REM ** READ DATA ITEM
440   T1$(I) = S$
450 NEXT I
460 RETURN

500 REM *** READ NUMBERS
510 FOR I = 1 TO T
520   GOSUB 2100 : REM ** BOT --- GARBAGE
530   FOR J = 1 TO V
540     GOSUB 2100 : REM ** DATA ITEM
550     T1(I,J) = V2
560   NEXT J
570 NEXT I
580 RETURN

600 REM *** WRITE NEW FILE
```

Figure 8.2: The DIF File Sorting Program (continues)

```
610 REM *** HEADER SECTION
620 V1 = 0 : S$ = ""
630 T$ = "TABLE" : V2 = 1 : GOSUB 3000
640 T$ = "VECTORS" : V2 = V : GOSUB 3000
650 T$ = "TUPLES" : V2 = T + 1 : GOSUB 3000
660 T$ = "DATA" : V2 = 0 : GOSUB 3000
670 REM *** STRING TUPLE
680 GOSUB 900 : REM ** BOT FLAG
690 V1 = 1 : V2 = 0
700 FOR I = 1 TO V
710    S$ = T1$(I) : GOSUB 3200
720 NEXT I
730 REM *** NUMERIC TUPLES
740 FOR I = 1 TO T
750    GOSUB 900 : REM ** BOT FLAG
755    V1 = 0 : S$ = "V"
760    FOR J = 1 TO V
770       V2 = T1(I,J) : GOSUB 3100
780    NEXT J
790 NEXT I
800 V1 = -1 : V2 = 0 : S$ = "EOD"
810 GOSUB 3100 : REM ** EOD FLAG
820 RETURN

900 REM *** WRITE BOT FLAG
910 V1 = -1 : V2 = 0 : S$ = "BOT" : GOSUB 3100
920 RETURN

1000 REM *** OPEN FILE FOR READING
        *** see Appendix A ***

1100 REM *** OPEN FILE FOR WRITING
        *** see Appendix A ***

1200 REM *** CLOSE FILE
        *** see Appendix A ***

2000 REM *** READ HEADER ITEM
        *** see Appendix A ***

2100 REM *** READ DATA ITEM
        *** see Appendix A ***

3000 REM *** WRITE HEADER ITEM
        *** see Appendix A ***

3100 REM *** WRITE DATA ITEM WITHOUT QUOTES
        *** see Appendix A ***

3200 REM *** WRITE DATA ITEM WITH QUOTES
        *** see Appendix A ***

4000 REM *** SORT THE FILE
4010 REM *** EITHER BY THE FIRST TUPLE
4020 REM *** OR THE LAST.
```

Figure 8.2: The DIF File Sorting Program (continues)

```
4030 FOR I = 1 TO V - 1
4040   FOR J = I + 1 TO V
4050     IF A$ = "A" THEN GOTO 4090
4060     REM ** NUMERIC SWAP
4070     IF T1(T,I) < T1(T,J) THEN GOSUB 4500
4080     GOTO 4110
4090     REM ** ALPHA SWAP
4100     IF T1$(I) > T1$(J) THEN GOSUB 4500
4110   NEXT J
4120 NEXT I
4130 RETURN
4500 REM *** SWAP ROUTINE
4510 H$ = T1$(I)
4520 T1$(I) = T1$(J)
4530 T1$(J) = H$
4540 FOR K = 1 TO T
4550   H = T1(K,I)
4560   T1(K,I) = T1(K,J)
4570   T1(K,J) = H
4580 NEXT K
4590 RETURN
```

Figure 8.2: The DIF File Sorting Program

active memory of the computer. The next message is actually another prompt:

A(LPHA OR N(UMERIC SORT?

In response to this prompt, you must type either an "A" or an "N" to indicate how you want the data to be sorted. The program will either sort the data alphabetically, by the first column of the labels, or numerically, by the last column of total values. We'll start by sorting the file alphabetically, as you can see in the sample dialogue.

After you have answered this prompt, you will see the message:

SORTING FILE.

The sorting process will not take very long with only ten rows of data, but if you later expand the rainfall spreadsheet to include more cities, the sort will take longer. When the sort is complete, another message will appear:

WRITING FILE.

At the same time your disk drive will activate, as the program saves the new DIF file on disk. When the saving process is finished, one last message will be printed on the screen:

* * * * * * * * * * * * * * * * * *

FILE ARAIN.DIF SAVED.

This message tells you some important facts about the action of the sort program. The program does *not* destroy your original, unsorted DIF file, RAIN.DIF. Instead, it creates a *new* file for the sorted version of RAIN.DIF. The program has a system for devising an easily recognizable name for the new file it creates. If you ask for an alphabetic sort, the program adds an "A" to the beginning of the original file name. Conversely, if you request a numeric sort, the new file name will begin with an "N". Thus, the name of the alphabetically sorted rainfall DIF file is ARAIN.DIF. If you now rerun the program and sort the file numerically, the program will produce the new file NRAIN.DIF.

Go ahead and type the program into your computer, store a copy of the program on disk, and run the program twice. First sort the DIF file alphabetically and then sort it numerically. When you have finished, look at your disk directory. All three of the following files should appear in the directory:

```
RAIN.DIF
ARAIN.DIF
NRAIN.DIF
```

Now let's return to the VisiCalc program to take a look at the new files we have created. We'll begin with ARAIN.DIF. Make sure you have the correct data disk in your disk drive, and type the following sequence of VisiCalc commands:

/S#	{invoke the DIF storage command}
L	{to **load** a DIF file}
ARAIN.DIF (return)	{enter the file name}
R	{to load the file by **rows**}
/GFI	{global integer format}

The results are shown in Figure 8.3. As you can see, the rows of data have, in fact, been sorted alphabetically by the names of the cities. Now clear the screen and inspect the numerically sorted file:

/CY	{clear the spreadsheet}
/S#	{invoke the DIF storage command}
L	{to **load** a DIF file}
NRAIN.DIF (return)	{enter the file name}
R	{to load by **rows**}
/GFI	{global integer format}

Scroll the window to the right until column N is in view. You will see that the rows of data have been sorted by the totals that appear in this column. The entire spreadsheet is shown in Figure 8.4.

	A	B	C	D	E	F	G
1	CLEVELND	7	6	8	9	9	8
2	DENVER	2	2	3	5	7	5
3	HONOLULU	11	6	8	4	3	1
4	LOS ANGL	8	7	6	3	0	0
5	MIAMI	6	5	5	9	15	23
6	NEW ORLN	11	12	14	11	11	12
7	NEW YORK	7	7	9	8	9	8
8	SAN FRAN	11	8	6	4	1	0
9	ST.LOUIS	5	5	8	10	10	11
10	WASH DC	7	6	8	7	10	9

	H	I	J	K	L	M	N
1	4	8	7	7	7	6	85
2	5	3	3	3	2	1	39
3	2	2	2	4	8	9	59
4	0	0	1	1	5	6	36
5	18	17	22	21	7	4	152
6	17	13	14	6	10	13	144
7	9	10	8	7	10	9	102
8	0	0	1	3	6	10	50
9	9	7	7	7	6	5	91
10	10	12	8	7	7	8	99

Figure 8.3: The Rainfall Spreadsheet Sorted Alphabetically

	A	B	C	D	E	F	G
1	MIAMI	6	5	5	9	15	23
2	NEW ORLN	11	12	14	11	11	12
3	NEW YORK	7	7	9	8	9	8
4	WASH DC	7	6	8	7	10	9
5	ST.LOUIS	5	5	8	10	10	11
6	CLEVELND	7	6	8	9	9	8
7	HONOLULU	11	6	8	4	3	1
8	SAN FRAN	11	8	6	4	1	0
9	DENVER	2	2	3	5	7	5
10	LOS ANGL	8	7	6	3	0	0

	H	I	J	K	L	M	N
1	18	17	22	21	7	4	152
2	17	13	14	6	10	13	144
3	9	10	8	7	10	9	102
4	10	12	8	7	7	8	99
5	9	7	7	7	6	5	91
6	4	8	7	7	7	6	85
7	2	2	2	4	8	9	59
8	0	0	1	3	6	10	50
9	5	3	3	3	2	1	39
10	0	0	1	1	5	6	36

Figure 8.4: The Rainfall Spreadsheet Sorted Numerically

So, we have seen that the entire sorting process, from the time you create the original DIF file from the VisiCalc spreadsheet, to the moment when you load the sorted DIF file back onto the screen, only takes a couple of minutes. The process is very simple, and the results are rather dramatic. What is even more important is that this process will work for *any* spreadsheet with any number of rows or columns, as long as it contains the two required columns of data—a first column of strings, and a final column of totals.

In the remaining sections of this chapter, we will take a close look at the BASIC program that performs this sorting task. Since the program is somewhat longer than the other two we have seen, we'll begin with an overview of the *structure* of the program before we look at its various subroutines in detail.

THE STRUCTURE OF THE PROGRAM

The diagram shown in Figure 8.5 is a *structure chart* of the DIF file sorting program. The purpose of this structure chart is to show graphically how the program is organized.

Each box in the structure chart represents one of the program's subroutines. The lines leading between the boxes represent subroutine calls. For example, you can see that the subroutine entitled "read strings" calls the subroutine entitled "read data item." The broken lines on the structure chart divide the subroutines into the three main tasks of the program—reading and storing the DIF data; sorting the data; and writing the new DIF file. The structure chart, then, is a tool that will help you see how the various subroutines work together. You should refer to it often as we discuss organization of the program.

The structure chart also gives a clear picture of the way the "main program" section controls the action of the program. Lines 10 to 250 make up the main program. The first half of this section (lines 10 to 130) is very similar to the main program of the statistics program in Chapter 7. This part of the main program does five things: it prints a title; it prompts you to enter the name of a DIF file; it opens the file; it reads the data into the arrays T1 and T1$; and, finally, it closes the file. The three subroutines that control the reading of the DIF file (at lines 300, 400, and 500) are identical to the subroutines used in the statistics program.

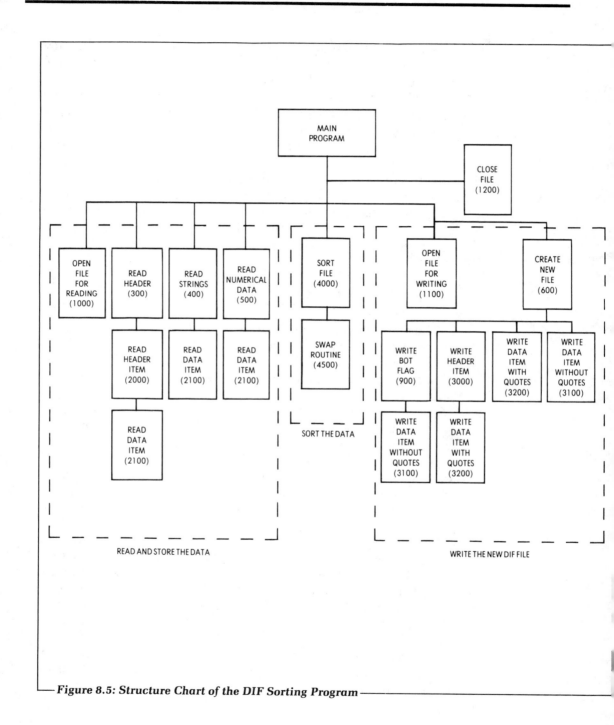

Figure 8.5: Structure Chart of the DIF Sorting Program

From line 140 on, however, this sort program takes on a personality of its own. Line 140 contains the INPUT instruction that asks you what kind of sort you want:

```
140 INPUT "A(LPHA OR N(UMERIC SORT?  "; A$
```

One of two characters must be read into the variable A$—"A" or "N". The logic of the sort subroutine depends on this. If, during a run of the program, you accidentally input some other character, then the program needs some way of alerting you to the error and making you repeat the input. Line 150 takes responsibility for checking your input:

```
150 IF A$ <> "A" AND A$ <> "N" THEN 140
```

If the character you have entered for A$ is neither "A" nor "N", line 150 sends control of the program back to line 140 again. The result of these two lines is that the prompt will be repeated until you enter a valid answer. For example:

```
A(LPHA OR N(UMERIC SORT? G

A(LPHA OR N(UMERIC SORT? M

A(LPHA OR N(UMERIC SORT? A
```

Once the program knows which kind of sort you want, it is ready to go to work. First, it determines the file name for the new DIF file it will be creating. You'll recall that it adds an "A" or an "N" to the front of the original file name. This is accomplished in line 160:

```
160 F$ = A$ + F$
```

This is an example of what is called *concatenation*—combining two strings to form a third string. Since A$ contains the sort code—"A" or "N"—the new F$ will contain the correct new file name.

The next several lines call the appropriate subroutines, and produce messages on the screen to tell you what is happening in the program. Line 180 calls the sort routine:

```
170 PRINT : PRINT "SORTING FILE."

180 GOSUB 4000
```

The new file is opened and written by the subroutine calls at lines 200 and 210, respectively:

```
190 PRINT : PRINT "WRITING FILE."

200 GOSUB 1100

210 GOSUB 600
```

And finally, after line 220 closes the file, lines 230 and 240 announce that the new sorted file has been created:

```
220 GOSUB 1200
230 PRINT : PRINT "*******************"
240 PRINT : PRINT "FILE "; F$; " SAVED."
```

The two subroutines that are new in this program are the sort subroutine (at line 4000) and the subroutine that creates (i.e., writes) the file (at line 600). We will examine these two routines with some care.

THE SORT SUBROUTINE

There are many different methods (or "algorithms," in computer programming parlance) for sorting a list of data. The method used in this program is not the most efficient in terms of run time, but it is by far the simplest. It is called the bubble sort. The technique of the bubble sort is to compare every element of the list, from top to bottom, with every element below it. If any two elements are found to be out of order, then they are exchanged ("swapped"). By the time the process reaches the bottom of the list, the sort is complete; all the elements are in order.

The comparisons are controlled by a pair of "nested" FOR loops in BASIC:

```
4030 FOR I = 1 TO V − 1
4040    FOR J = I + 1 TO V
        ...

        (compare elements, and swap if necessary)
        ...

4110    NEXT J
4120 NEXT I
```

You can see that these FOR loops are designed to cover all V vectors of the data. Since our data is stored in arrays, the variables I and J (which are incremented by the FOR loops) become the indices into the arrays.

What adds complexity to the sort subroutine is that it must be able to sort either numerically or alphabetically, depending on the value of the sort code variable, A$. For this reason, the instructions inside the two loops are divided into two logical parts. Line

4050 determines which set of instructions will be executed:

    4050 IF A$ = "A" THEN GOTO 4090

The alphabetic sort requires comparisons of the string array, T1$. If two elements of this array are out of order, the *entire rows* that they represent must be swapped. To simplify this procedure, the swapping itself is performed by another subroutine altogether, at line 4500. Line 4100 calls this routine if its comparison shows that two elements of T1$ are out of order:

    4100 IF T1$(I) > T1$(J) THEN GOSUB 4500

Likewise, the numeric sort must call the swap routine if two elements of the *last* column of data are out of order. This last column is accessed via the value of the variable T—the number of *numeric* tuples. (You'll recall that the subroutine at line 300 determines this value from the TUPLES item of the header.) The numeric sort comparisons are made in line 4070:

    4070 IF T1(T,I) < T1(T,J) THEN GOSUB 4500

If a numeric sort is being performed, then the program must skip over the instructions that carry out the alphabetic sort. This is the reason for the GOTO instruction in line 4080:

    4080 GOTO 4110

If you have trouble catching on right away to the logic of the bubble sort, try to think of the arrays T1 and T1$ as a single two dimensional table—like a spreadsheet table. Think of comparing elements down a column—either the string column or the total column—and making exchanges when necessary. But remember, when you exchange two elements, it's not sufficient just to make the swap within the column whose elements you are comparing. You must exchange the *entire rows* represented by those two elements. This is the job of the swap routine, at line 4500.

The swap routine has two sections. The first section, at lines 4510 to 4530, is for swapping the strings of the one-dimensional array T1$. There are three steps to the swap process. First, one of the two elements must be assigned temporarily to a "holding" variable, H$:

    4510 H$ = T1$(I)

Then the position of the first element can be assigned a new value—the value of the second element:

```
4520 T1$(I) = T1$(J)
```

And finally the value stored in H$ becomes the new second element:

```
4530 T1$(J) = H$
```

The second section of the swap routine is for the numeric swap. This swap is also performed in three steps. However, since two whole *rows* of elements must be exchanged, the swap is performed within a FOR loop:

```
4540 FOR K = 1 TO T
4550    H = T1(K,I)
4560    T1(K,I) = T1(K,J)
4570    T1(K,J) = H
4580 NEXT K
```

In terms of programming time, the bubble sort is very economical. Even with the added complexity of choosing between numeric and alphabetic sorts, the entire operation is performed in fewer than twenty lines of BASIC code. This is why the bubble sort is so popular. However, it also has its disadvantages. It becomes slower and slower as the size of the array increases. If you find that you are using the sort program for large VisiCalc spreadsheets, you might want to investigate other sorting algorithms. To revise the sorting method, you only need to change the sort subroutine itself. The swap subroutine will remain the same.

THE DIF FILE CREATION SUBROUTINE

Once the array has been sorted, the subroutine at line 600 takes over to write the sorted data to a new DIF file. With one important exception, the writing is simply the reverse of the reading process. When we read the DIF file, we first called the reading subroutines, and then accessed the variables into which the DIF data had been read. Now, to write a DIF file, we will start by assigning values to the appropriate variables; *then* we will call the writing subroutines, which write the values of those variables to the file.

The exceptional difference between the two processes is this: In reading the DIF file we could treat any data that didn't interest us as garbage. But to write a DIF file correctly we must systematically keep track of each element of the DIF format, and include those elements one by one in the file.

You'll recall that our library of file-handling subroutines contains three routines for writing files. The subroutine at line 3000 writes a header item. The subroutines at lines 3100 and 3200 both write data items, the former without string quotes, and the latter with them. The variables that these subroutines use are the same ones used by the file reading subroutines—T$, for header titles; V1, and V2 for numeric data; and S$ for string data. So it is to these four variables that we will have to assign values before each call to a file-writing subroutine.

The subroutine at line 600 is divided into three parts. The first part (lines 610 to 660) writes the header section. The second part (lines 670 to 720) and the third part (lines 730 to 790) write the data section, first the tuple of strings and then the numeric tuples. Let's look at these three parts one at a time.

The values of V1 and S$ are constant for all the items of the header section. Line 620 assigns these values:

```
620 V1 = 0 : S$ = ""
```

Then the next four lines write each of the four items of the header section. Each line assigns new values to T$ and V2 and then calls the subroutine at 3000 to write the item. Notice that the values of V and T + 1 provide the number of vectors and tuples, respectively:

```
640 T$ = "VECTORS" : V2 = V : GOSUB 3000
650 T$ = "TUPLES" : V2 = T + 1 : GOSUB 3000
```

Each of the tuples in the data section of the file must begin with a BOT flag. The subroutine at 900 is designed to write that flag. It assigns the appropriate values, and calls the subroutine at 3100 to write the item:

```
910 V1 = −1 : V2 = 0 : S$ = "BOT" : GOSUB 3100
```

The second part of the file creation subroutine writes the string tuple. It begins with a call to the BOT flag subroutine:

```
680 GOSUB 900
```

Then it assigns values to V1 and V2. Remember that the type identifier for string items is 1:

```
690 V1 = 1 : V2 = 0
```

Finally, it uses a FOR loop to assign each value of the array T1$ to S$ and then write the item:

```
700 FOR I = 1 TO V
710    S$ = T1$(I) : GOSUB 3200
720 NEXT I
```

Notice that the subroutine at 3200 is used to write the string items. This subroutine puts quotes around the value of S$.

The third part of this subroutine writes the numeric tuples. It uses a pair of nested loops to do the job. The outer loop creates each tuple, starting with a BOT flag:

```
740 FOR I = 1 TO T
750 GOSUB 900
```

The type identifier for numeric data is 0; this value is assigned to V1, and "V" is assigned to the string variable S$:

```
755 V1 = 0 : S$ = "V"
```

Then the inner loop assigns values from the array T1 to the variable V2, and writes each data item to the file:

```
760 FOR J = 1 TO V
770    V2 = T1(I,J) : GOSUB 3100
780 NEXT J
```

One detail remains before the file can be called complete. The last two lines of the subroutine write the EOD flag:

```
800 V1 = −1 : V2 = 0 : S$ = "EOD"
810 GOSUB 3100
```

All in all, this subroutine shows that writing a DIF file is only a little harder than reading one. As with all programming tasks, the key is careful organization, and judicious use of subroutines.

SUMMARY

The ultimate goal in the VisiCalc/BASIC relationship is to go full circle with data processing—from VisiCalc, to BASIC, and then back to VisiCalc again. As we have seen in the sort program, the DIF file is an excellent medium for moving data around this circle efficiently and reliably.

APPENDIX A:

FILE-HANDLING SUBROUTINES FOR THREE POPULAR PERSONAL COMPUTERS

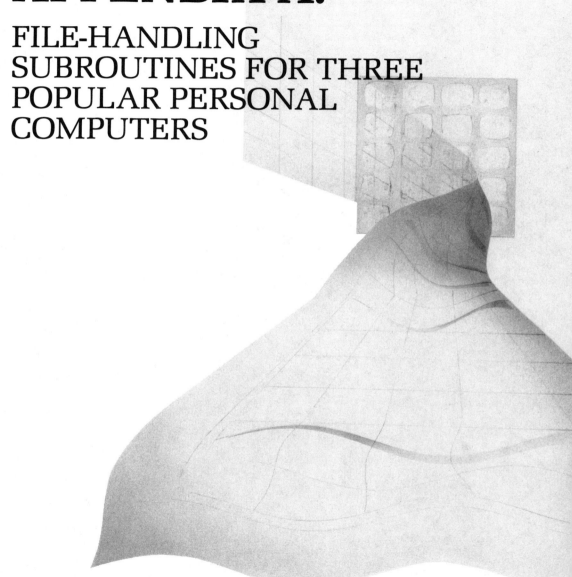

INTRODUCTION

The subroutines listed in this appendix are designed specifically for the file-handling requirements of the BASIC programs in Chapters 6, 7, and 8. For a general discription of the action of these routines, see Figure 6.7 in Chapter 6.

Sequential files may be opened either for input or for output. If you are writing to a file and you subsequently want to read from the same file, you must first close the file and then reopen it for reading. The programs in Chapter 6 and 7 simply read data files, so they only need one subroutine to open a file for reading. The program in Chapter 8, however, reads one file, closes it, and later opens a different file for writing. This program, then, requires two different subroutines for opening files, one to open for reading, and another to open for writing. The BASIC instructions for the two operations are not the same.

When a program is reading a sequential file, *each* data item of the file must be read, item by item, from the beginning of the file, even if the reading program has no need for certain items. As a result, the programs in Chapters 6, 7, and 8 read many items as "garbage"—i.e., items that are read and then discarded.

APPLE® BASIC

Figure A.1 shows the subroutines for Applesoft disk BASIC. In this version of BASIC, the control-D character is used to alert the operating system to the fact that a DOS command is going to be executed from within the BASIC program. The ASCII code for control-D is 4; this is designated by CHR$(4) in the subroutines. Thus, the OPEN, CLOSE, READ, and WRITE commands are all executed by PRINT statements that begin with control-D. Two PRINT statements are required for opening a sequential file—one for the OPEN command, and one for the READ or WRITE command. For example:

```
1010 D$ = CHR$(4)
1020 PRINT D$; "OPEN "; F$
1030 PRINT D$; "READ "; F$
```

After the file is opened for reading, any subsequent INPUT

instructions read data *from the file*. Likewise, when a file is opened for writing, any PRINT instructions write data *to the file*.

```
1000 REM *** OPEN FILE FOR READING
1010 D$ = CHR$(4) : REM ** CONTROL-D
1020 PRINT D$; "OPEN "; F$
1030 PRINT D$; "READ "; F$
1040 RETURN

1100 REM *** OPEN FILE FOR WRITING
1110 D$ = CHR$(4) : REM ** CONTROL-D
1120 PRINT D$; "OPEN "; F$
1130 PRINT D$; "WRITE "; F$
1140 RETURN

1200 REM *** CLOSE FILE
1210 PRINT D$; "CLOSE"
1220 RETURN

2000 REM *** READ HEADER ITEM
2010 INPUT T$
2020 GOSUB 2100
2030 RETURN

2100 REM *** READ DATA ITEM
2110 INPUT V1, V2
2120 INPUT S$
2130 RETURN

3000 REM *** WRITE HEADER ITEM
3010 PRINT T$
3020 GOSUB 3200
3030 RETURN

3100 REM *** WRITE DATA ITEM WITHOUT QUOTES
3110 PRINT V1; ","; V2
3120 PRINT S$
3130 RETURN

3200 REM *** WRITE DATA ITEM WITH QUOTES
3210 PRINT V1; ","; V2
3220 PRINT CHR$(34); S$; CHR$(34)
3230 RETURN
```

Figure A.1: File-Handling Subroutines in Applesoft BASIC

TRS-80™ BASIC

Figure A.2 shows the same subroutines for TRS-80 BASIC. The OPEN command takes three parameters. The first, either "I" or "O", indicates whether the file is being opened for input or output. The second, an integer from 1 to 15, assigns the file to a *memory buffer*, which stores data temporarily while it is on its way to or from the disk file. The third parameter is the file name.

So, the command:

    1010 OPEN "I", 1, F$

opens file F$ for input (i.e., reading) and assigns it to buffer #1. The statement:

    1110 OPEN "O", 2, F$

opens file F$ for output and assigns it to file buffer #2.

The INPUT# and PRINT# statements are used for file input and output. They must include the buffer number of the file that is being read or written. For example:

    2010 INPUT#1, T$

reads a string value from the file assigned to buffer #1.

```
1000 REM *** OPEN FILE FOR READING
1010 OPEN "I", 1, F$
1020 RETURN

1100 REM *** OPEN FILE FOR WRITING
1110 OPEN "O", 2, F$
1120 RETURN

1200 REM *** CLOSE FILE
1210 CLOSE
1220 RETURN

2000 REM *** READ HEADER ITEM
2010 INPUT#1, T$
2020 GOSUB 2100
2030 RETURN

2100 REM *** READ DATAITEM
2110 INPUT#1, V1, V2
2120 INPUT#1, S$
2130 RETURN

3000 REM *** WRITE HEADER ITEM
3010 PRINT#2, T$
3020 GOSUB 3200
3030 RETURN

3100 REM *** WRITE DATA ITEM WITHOUT QUOTES
3110 PRINT#2, V1; ","; V2
3120 PRINT#2, S$
3130 RETURN

3200 REM *** WRITE DATA ITEM WITH QUOTES
3210 PRINT#2, V1; ","; V2
3220 PRINT#2, CHR$(34); S$; CHR$(34)
3230 RETURN
```

Figure A.2: File-Handling Subroutines for the TRS-80

IBM® PERSONAL COMPUTER BASIC

The file subroutines for the IBM Personal Computer, shown in Figure A.3, are similar to those for the TRS-80. The IBM Personal Computer allows two different versions of the open statement. For example, the following two statements both perform the same task of opening the file F$ for input and assigning it to buffer #1:

```
1010 OPEN F$ FOR INPUT AS #1
1010 OPEN "I", #1, F$
```

The subroutines of Figure A.3 use the first of these two statements, since its meaning is clearer than that of the second version.

```
1000 REM *** OPEN FILE FOR READING
1010 OPEN F$ FOR INPUT AS #1
1020 RETURN

1100 REM *** OPEN FILE FOR WRITING
1110 OPEN F$ FOR OUTPUT AS #2
1120 RETURN

1200 REM *** CLOSE FILE
1210 CLOSE
1220 RETURN

2000 REM *** READ HEADER ITEM
2010 INPUT#1, T$
2020 GOSUB 2100
2030 RETURN

2100 REM *** READ DATA ITEM
2110 INPUT#1, V1, V2
2120 INPUT#1, S$
2130 RETURN

3000 REM *** WRITE HEADER ITEM
3010 PRINT#2, T$
3020 GOSUB 3200
3030 RETURN

3100 REM *** WRITE DATA ITEM WITHOUT QUOTES
3110 PRINT #2, V1; ","; V2
3120 PRINT #2, S$
3130 RETURN

3200 REM *** WRITE DATA ITEM WITH QUOTES
3210 PRINT#2, V1; ","; V2
3220 PRINT#2, CHR$(34); S$; CHR$(34)
3230 RETURN
```

Figure A.3: File-Handling Subroutines for the IBM Personal Computer

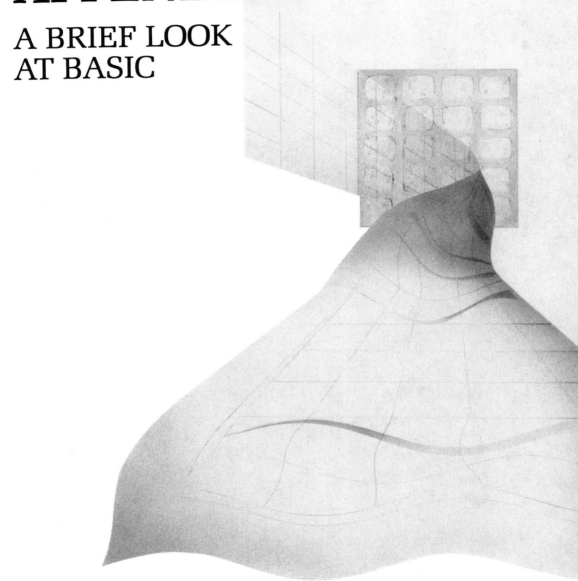

APPENDIX B:

A BRIEF LOOK
AT BASIC

INTRODUCTION

The purpose of this appendix is to help you understand the three BASIC programs developed in this book. It is not a complete introduction to the BASIC language, but will at least get you started if you have had little or no experience with BASIC programming. The ideal time to read this appendix is after you have completed the first five chapters of the book, and before you begin the last three.

In this appendix, as we study the instructions of BASIC, we will often compare them to the features of the VisiCalc program. We will note many similarities between the two programming tools, as well as a few important differences.

Important points of comparison between VisiCalc and BASIC will be summarized in boldface type in this appendix.

There are two reasons for comparing the features of VisiCalc and BASIC:

1. You will probably find that your new familiarity with the VisiCalc program will help you "visualize" some of the concepts of BASIC programming, thus making it easier for you to learn BASIC.

2. In order to use both VisiCalc and BASIC most effectively, you must learn enough about their respective characteristics to recognize the ideal time to use one or the other.

This second reason is one of the themes developed in Chapters 6, 7, and 8; but this appendix will fill you in on some of the technical details involved in the discussion.

WHAT IS A BASIC PROGRAM?

A BASIC program is a numbered sequence of instructions designed to make your computer accomplish a job. The instructions must all be written in the limited and specific vocabulary and syntax that compose the BASIC language. The lines of a program are numbered in ascending order, although the numbering system does not necessarily have to be in regular multiples. For example, the first lines of a program could be numbered:

        1
        2
        3
        4
        5
or:
        10
        20
        30
        40
        50
or even:
        10
        13
        20
        25
        37

All that matters is that the numbers *increase* from the beginning to the end of the program. A program can be any length that suits the job it has to perform—from one line to several hundred lines.

The instructions of a numbered BASIC program produce no immediate results when you first type them into your computer. This is one aspect of a BASIC program that is essentially different from a sequence of VisiCalc commands. In VisiCalc, you see immediate results almost each time you enter a command onto the spreadsheet. You may see new data, new calculations, or new formats—but something visual will happen on the screen. In BASIC, on the other hand, you must give the operating system of your computer a specific command when you want to run the program. Usually, the way you do this is simply by entering the word:

        RUN

while your program resides in the active memory of your computer. The computer then executes each of the commands of your BASIC program, one by one, in the order specified by the logic of the program itself.

One essential difference between BASIC and VisiCalc, then, is that VisiCalc commands are generally carried out as soon as you enter them, whereas the commands of a BASIC program are not executed until you run the whole program.

A line in a BASIC program may actually contain more than one instruction. Different instructions on the same line are separated by a colon (:). For example, the following line contains three different instructions:

```
630 T$ = "TABLE" : V2 = 1 : GOSUB 3000
```

Some versions of BASIC use the backslash character (\) rather than the colon to separate different instructions on a line.

A display of all the lines of a program is called a *listing*. A listing can appear either on the screen of your computer or on páper. Often you'll want to include a certain amount of documentation about a program within the listing itself. You may want to indicate where one section of a program ends and where another begins. Or you may want to describe exactly what a certain line does. The REM instruction (for *remark*) allows you to do all this. When you write REM as the first word of a line, BASIC ignores anything that appears thereafter on that line. For example, at the beginning of a program you might include lines that describe the purpose of the program:

```
10 REM ✶✶✶ THIS PROGRAM DISPLAYS
20 REM ✶✶✶ A DIF FILE
30 REM ✶✶✶ ON YOUR SCREEN.
```

There is no restriction on the words or symbols that you write after REM. You may write anything that you think might be helpful to someone who is trying to use or understand your program. You can also use REM as the last instruction on a line that contains more than one instruction. For example:

```
70 GOSUB 1000 : REM ✶✶ OPEN FILE
```

The BASIC word END is the final instruction of a program. END tells the computer that the program is finished. (However, END does not necessarily have to appear on the final *line* of a BASIC program. We will see why this is true when we study how execution of a program is controlled.)

Finally, when you write a BASIC program you'll probably want to save it on disk so that you can use it more than once. BASIC programs can be saved on disk and then "loaded" back into the active memory of your computer, just as VisiCalc programs can. Your operating system will supply its own specific commands for creating a BASIC program file on disk. You should find out what these commands are *before* you start writing programs that are important enough to save.

STORING DATA IN BASIC

In the VisiCalc program, each position on the spreadsheet can hold one item of data. BASIC also has structures that store single items of data. They are called *variables*. The reason for this term is that the value stored in a variable can change during the course of a program. Each variable has a name; it is referred to by the same name each time it is used. Many versions of BASIC limit the length of variable names to one, two, or three characters. The first character must be a letter from A to Z. Some examples of variable names in these BASICs are:

V1

V2

I

J

N

Other BASICs allow variable names to be longer. The advantage to this is that you can write names that express the nature of the data that the variables actually store. For example:

VALUE1

VALUE2

The programs presented in this book use short variable names so that they will be acceptable to the most common versions of BASIC. If you have a BASIC that allows long variable names, however, you should take advantage of this feature, since meaningful names make a program easier to read and understand.

Unlike the positions on your VisiCalc spreadsheet, a given BASIC variable is defined to hold one specific *type* of data item. The type of data that a variable can store is identified by the last character of the name of the variable. If the last character of a name is $, then the variable is defined for storing strings. (Non-numeric data—known as *labels* in VisiCalc—are called *strings* in BASIC.) Some examples of string variable names are:

    T$
    S$
    A$

A name ending in the character % designates an integer variable:

    I%
    J%

Finally, if a variable name ends in a letter or a digit, rather than one of the two special characters ($ or %), then it designates a *real-number* variable. (A real number is one that can contain a decimal fraction.)

Don't confuse BASIC variable names with VisiCalc addresses. In VisiCalc, when we refer to an address such as M5 we are talking about a position on the spreadsheet—specifically, the position at the intersection of column M and row 5. A BASIC variable could also be named M5, but the individual characters of this variable name have no special meaning to BASIC. As a BASIC programmer, you will choose variable names that help you to remember what the variables represent. For example, M5 might mean "month #5" to you. But to BASIC, M5 is just another variable name.

A BASIC variable, like a position on the VisiCalc spreadsheet, stores one item of data. The type of data a variable can store is indicated in the last character of the variable name itself. Otherwise, variable names are chosen for their significance to the programmer, not for their significance to BASIC.

The BASIC instruction that stores an item of data in a variable is called an *assignment statement*, because it assigns a value to the variable. An example of an assignment statement is:

    10 V1 = 1

This statement means, "Store the value 1 in the variable V1." The "verb" of an assignment statement is always represented by the equal sign (=). Only a single variable name may appear at the left of the equal sign. At the right of the equal sign, however, more complex expressions are legal. For example:

    205 V2 = T + 1

This statement involves two variables, V2, and T. The statement says: "Add 1 to the value of T and store the sum in V2." When the instruction is executed, only the variable V2 will receive a new value. The variable T, on the right side of the equal sign, will not change.

Many times in BASIC programming the name of a variable will appear on both sides of the equal sign. When you see this kind of assignment statement, you will know that a new value is being calculated for the variable at the left of the equal sign, but in a special way. The calculation of the new value will be based partly on the old value of the variable. Here is an example:

$$215 \; V1 = V1 + 1$$

This statement says, "Add 1 to the current value of V1, and then store the sum in V1." Or, more simply, "Increment the value of V1 by 1." In this case, since V1 can only store one value at a time, the old value of V1 is lost.

There is no limit to the complexity of the arithmetic on the right side of an assignment statement. BASIC computes the value of the expression on the right and assigns the result to the variable on the left. The symbols used for arithmetic operations are the same as in the VisiCalc program:

+ addition
− subtraction
* multiplication
/ division
^ exponentiation

The *order* in which these operations are evaluated, however, is *not* the same as the VisiCalc program. VisiCalc, you'll recall, simply evaluates arithmetic expressions from left to right. BASIC, on the other hand, always respects a fixed hierarchy of operations. Here is the order in which operations are evaluated:

1. exponentiation
2. multiplication and division (from left to right)
3. addition and subtraction (from left to right)

For example, consider the expression on the right side of the following assignment statement:

$$100 \; V1 = A + B * C^D$$

The expression, as written, would be evaluated from right to left, following the hierarchy of operations—first exponentiation, then multiplication, then addition.

Just as in VisiCalc, however, you can change the order of operations by adding parentheses to an arithmetic expression:

```
100 V1 = ((A + B) * C)^D
```

With these parentheses, the expression would be evaluated from left to right—starting with the inner-most parentheses and moving outward.

VisiCalc and BASIC have two different systems for evaluating arithmetic expressions. For this reason, you must write such expressions very carefully to avoid unexpected, and unpleasant, results.

ARRAYS IN BASIC

In addition to the simple variable, BASIC has another, more complex, structure for storing data. This structure is the *array*. An array stores *groups* of data items in a way that is very similar to the rows and columns of the VisiCalc spreadsheet.

Before you begin using an array in a BASIC program, though, you must explicitly specify three characteristics of the array: type, dimension, and length. BASIC has a special statement that is used just to define these array characteristics. It is the DIM statement (for *dimension*). Here is an example:

```
20 DIM T1$(10), T1(12,10)
```

This DIM statement defines two arrays. The first array is named T1$. Its name declares it as an array of strings; that is, every data item stored in T1$ will be a string. (The conventions for declaring variable types in the names of variables also apply to arrays.) The number 10, in parentheses after the name, specifies the *length* of the array. Specifically, it tells us that T1$ is defined to store 11 data items—numbered 0 to 10. T1$ is a one-dimensional array; only one number appears between the parentheses.

The array T1 is a two-dimensional array of real numbers. Since the lengths of its two dimensions are specified as 12 and 10, respectively, we know that the array can hold a table of real numbers that is 13 items long (0 to 12) by 11 items wide (0 to 10).

When you assign values to an array you must specify precisely where in the array the values are to be stored. For example, the following statements assign string values to all eleven elements of the array T1$:

```
10 T1$(0)  = "ZERO"
15 T1$(1)  = "ONE"
20 T1$(2)  = "TWO"
25 T1$(3)  = "THREE"
30 T1$(4)  = "FOUR"
35 T1$(5)  = "FIVE"
40 T1$(6)  = "SIX"
45 T1$(7)  = "SEVEN"
50 T1$(8)  = "EIGHT"
55 T1$(9)  = "NINE"
60 T1$(10) = "TEN"
```

You can also use a *variable* to specify a place in an array. If, for example, you have assigned the value 5 to a variable named I, say in line 20 of your program, then the statement:

```
30 T1$(I) = "FIVE"
```

assigns a string to the fifth element (I = 5) of T1$. The variable I in this example is called the *index* into the array T1$.

A one-dimensional array in BASIC is like a row or column on the VisiCalc spreadsheet; it stores a list of data items. A two-dimensional array stores a table of data items. However, any given BASIC array is limited to one specific type of data.

INPUT AND OUTPUT IN BASIC

When you use the VisiCalc program you tend not to think of input and output as two distinct processes, because they actually occur simultaneously. If you are creating a table of numbers, for example, you can see the table developing *as* you enter the values. If you then type a formula to calculate a new value for the table, you see the results of the formula immediately.

In BASIC, on the other hand, you are much more likely to distinguish clearly between the process of inputting data into the program and the subsequent process of outputting the results. In fact, BASIC has two distinct sets of commands that deal with input and output. As a BASIC programmer, you have to use these commands to tell your program specifically how, when, and where to read and write data.

There are three possible sources of input data for a BASIC program. The simplest and most static source is the program itself. For example, you might use an assignment statement to make a certain data value available to your BASIC program:

```
100 P1 = 3.14
```

The disadvantage of writing data directly into your program is that you have to change the program itself in order to revise the data. This is not a reasonable approach when a program needs lots of data that is likely to be different each time the program is run.

A much better approach—and one that microcomputer BASICs are particularly well designed for—is to instruct your program to read data from the keyboard. In effect, then, you can design a BASIC program that "talks" to the person who is sitting at the computer, and receives information back again from that person via the keyboard. We often refer to this two-way communication as a *dialogue* between the BASIC program and the user of the program. You must design all the details of this dialogue in advance as though you were writing a scene for a play.

The primary BASIC instruction that you can use to conduct such dialogues is the INPUT statement. The implementation details of the INPUT statement may vary slightly from one version of BASIC to another, but essentially this command performs three tasks:

1. It displays a "prompt" on the screen of the computer. This prompt is usually a question or a declarative sentence that indicates to the user what data item to enter. You plan this prompt yourself when you write the INPUT statement.

2. It reads the data item that the user types at the keyboard in response to the prompt.

3. It assigns that data item to a specified variable.

The following example illustrates these three tasks:

```
50 INPUT "HOW OLD ARE YOU? "; Y%
```

This line has three different elements: first, the command word itself: INPUT; second, the prompt, written between quotation marks; and third, the name of the variable that is to store the input data. When BASIC executes this line, it will begin by displaying the prompt on the screen:

HOW OLD ARE YOU?

and then it will wait for a response to be typed at the keyboard. Let's say the user enters the number 31 in response to the prompt question:

HOW OLD ARE YOU? 31

The input value 31 will be stored in the variable Y%. Any time the program subsequently needs to use this input item, it can find it in Y%.

You can, of course, use the INPUT statement to read string data as well as numerical data. The following statement reads a string into the variable N$:

40 INPUT "WHAT IS YOUR NAME? "; N$

For output of data to the screen, BASIC supplies the PRINT command. PRINT can be used in a number of different ways. Again, different versions of BASIC offer a variety of different features that work with the PRINT command. The simplest use of PRINT is to display the current value of a variable on the screen. The statement:

60 PRINT Y%

would display whatever value is stored in the variable Y%. You can also include explicit strings in a PRINT statement, which is valuable when you want to display output data in an explanatory context. For example:

60 PRINT "YOU ARE "; Y%; " YEARS OLD."

This statement includes the value of Y% in a sentence displayed on the screen. If the current value stored in Y% is 31, then this PRINT statement will produce the following line of output:

YOU ARE 31 YEARS OLD.

The punctuation in a PRINT statement is always significant. The semicolon (;) is used to separate different data elements in a PRINT statement, as in line 60 above. The comma, on the other hand, performs an additional function. You can use a comma separator in the PRINT command to create columns of data. For example, let's say the variables V1, V2, V3, V4, V5, and V6 contain the integer values 1 to 6, respectively. Then the statements:

```
70 PRINT V1, V2, V3
80 PRINT V4, V5, V6
```

will produce the following lines:

```
1       2       3
4       5       6
```

The space separating the columns, and the number of columns across the screen, both depend on the version of BASIC you are using.

Many BASICs have a function called TAB, which will also produce columnar output results. The TAB function instructs BASIC to output data at a certain line-position on the screen. For example, the lines:

```
90 PRINT TAB(10); V1; TAB(20); V2
100 PRINT TAB(10); V3; TAB(20); V4
```

produce two columns of data as follows:

```
1       2
3       4
```

The first column is 10 spaces away from the left border of the screen, and the two columns are separated by 10 spaces.

Finally, the PRINT USING command supplies, for versions of BASIC that have it, a means of formatting the output of numeric data. PRINT USING takes directions from a string consisting of special characters (including "#", "$", "*", ".", and ",") to format a number for output. For some examples and an explanation of the use of this command, see Figure B.1.

BASIC has some screen-output features that are similar to the VisiCalc global format commands. These features include the TAB function, which is a tool for producing columns of data, and PRINT USING, for formatting numeric data. In general, however, input and output must be planned much more explicitly in BASIC than in VisiCalc.

The third source of data for a BASIC program is an external data file, stored on disk or cassette tape. The syntax of the file input and output commands tends to vary widely from one version of

```
STATEMENTS                              OUTPUT RESULTS

10 V1 = 1532.14
20 PRINT USING "$$##,###.##"; V1        $1,532.14

----------------------------------------------------------------

10 V1 = 23456.789
20 S$ = "PAY EXACTLY **$##,####.##"
30 PRINT USING S$; V1                   PAY EXACTLY ***$23,456.79

----------------------------------------------------------------

10 V1 = 1.234
20 V2 = 25.71
30 V3 = 98.7654
40 S$ = "###.#    ###.#    ###.#"
50 PRINT USING S$; V1, V2, V3           1.2    25.7    98.8
```

#	Represents one digit of the number
.	Indicates placement of decimal point
,	Causes commas to be printed every three digits to the left of the decimal; may be placed in any position in the format string
$	Puts dollar signs in position indicated
$$	Places "floating" dollar sign
**	Fills space up to the first digit with asterisks
**$	Prints asterisks before floating dollar sign

Figure B.1: Examples and Explanation of PRINT USING

BASIC to another. Appendix A shows examples of these commands for three different BASICs.

In terms of the way data is accessed, there are two different kinds of data files—sequential access and random access. The data items of a sequential access file must be read from top to bottom, item by item. In other words, if you want to access the tenth item of a sequential data file, you must first read the first nine items, even if those nine elements are of no relevance whatsoever to the task before you. Sequential access files are suitable for large data processing tasks that involve storage and access of many similar data items.

The data items of random access files may be read in any order. Often a random access file is used in conjunction with an indexing structure that facilitates retrieval of specific data from the file.

CONTROLLING A BASIC PROGRAM

Even though a BASIC program is numbered in ascending order, the numbering system does not necessarily represent the order in which the lines of the program will be executed. Many times it suits the logic of a particular task to skip forward to a line further down in the program, or to jump backward to a line further up. Often you'll want to execute the same line or set of lines more than once. BASIC supplies different kinds of commands that allow you, the programmer, to control the order of execution of the lines in a program. The commands are GOTO, GOSUB, and FOR/NEXT. We will examine each of these commands in turn in this section.

THE GOTO COMMAND
AND THE IF STATEMENT

The GOTO statement sends control of the program to a specific line number. The direction of the jump can be forward or backward. The following statement, located at line 10, directs the program to jump forward to line 100:

    10 GOTO 100

This statement orders a backward jump:

    200 GOTO 150

When BASIC encounters a GOTO statement, it immediately jumps to the specified line number and executes the command in that line. Then, it moves forward from that new point in the program.

Don't confuse the BASIC GOTO statement with the VisiCalc GO TO command (>). They have nothing at all in common. The BASIC GOTO is used to direct the order of execution of the lines of a program. The VisiCalc GO TO simply repositions the VisiCalc cursor to a new place on the spreadsheet.

The action of the GOTO statement can be made *conditional*, by combining it with the IF statement in BASIC. For example:

    50 IF I > 0 THEN GOTO 10

This statement says, "If the value of the variable I is greater than 0 then send control of the program back to line 10; otherwise, proceed forward as usual."

Like VisiCalc, the BASIC language includes a whole vocabulary devoted to logical statements. In addition to IF, BASIC has the words AND, OR, and NOT, and the logical operators $>$, $<$, $>=$, $<=$, $=$, and $<>$, which are conceptually the same as the equivalent features in the VisiCalc program. However, there is an important difference between the action of a VisiCalc logical function and the potential range of results possible from BASIC logical statements:

In the VisiCalc program an @IF function simply chooses between two different values, and stores one of them in a specified spreadsheet position. In BASIC, however, the resulting action of an IF statement can be expressed by almost any BASIC command, including PRINT, INPUT, GOTO, GOSUB, or an assignment statement.

Figure B.2 shows some examples of IF statements in BASIC. Read them and see if you can describe what the result of each one would be.

```
10 V1 = 0
20 V2 = 10000
30 INPUT "TYPE A NUMBER "; X
40 IF (X < V1) THEN PRINT "THE NUMBER IS NEGATIVE"
50 IF (X >= V1) AND (X <= V2) THEN PRINT "BETWEEN";V1;"AND";V2
60 IF (X > V2) PRINT "LARGE NUMBER"
70 IF (X < V1) OR (X > V2) THEN PRINT "NEGATIVE OR VERY LARGE"
80 IF NOT (X = V1) THEN PRINT "NOT EQUAL TO ";V1
90 IF (X <> V2) THEN PRINT "NOT EQUAL TO ";V2
100 END
```

— *Figure B.2: Examples of the IF Statement in BASIC* —

THE GOSUB STATEMENT

The GOSUB statement in BASIC passes control of the program to a subroutine. We say that the GOSUB command "calls" a subroutine. A subroutine is a group of lines that are designed to perform a certain task. When the task is complete, the subroutine *returns* control of the program back to the line following the subroutine call. Here is a short, and somewhat whimsical, example of a program that contains subroutines:

```
10 REM *** PERSONAL INFORMATION
20 INPUT "HOW OLD ARE YOU? "; Y%
30 IF (Y% >= 17) AND (Y% < 21) THEN GOSUB 100
40 IF Y% < 17 THEN GOSUB 200
50 IF Y% >= 21 THEN GOSUB 300
60 INPUT "WHAT IS YOUR NAME? "; N$
70 GOSUB 1000 : REM ** PROCESS THE DATA
80 END

100 REM ** YOUNG ADULT
110 INPUT "DO YOU W(ORK OR GO TO S(CHOOL <W OR S>? "; A$
120 IF (A$ <> "S") AND (A$ <> "W") THEN GOTO 110
130 IF A$ = "S" THEN GOSUB 200
140 IF A$ = "W" THEN GOSUB 300
150 RETURN

200 REM ** CHILD
210 INPUT "WHERE DO YOU GO TO SCHOOL? "; S$
220 RETURN

300 REM ** ADULT
310 INPUT "WHERE DO YOU WORK? "; W$
320 INPUT "WHAT IS YOUR JOB? "; J$
330 RETURN

1000 REM ** PROCESS DATA
1010 REM
1020 REM -- THIS SUBROUTINE IS NOT WRITTEN YET --
1030 RETURN
```

Figure B.3: Structure Chart of the "Personal Information" Program

This program is designed to gather information about a person and then to process the information in some way. The program puts people into three age categories: children, under age 17, who go to school; young adults, from 17 to 20, who might either work or go to school; and adults, age 21 or over, who work. (This oversimplification of reality is, of course, merely for the sake of illustration.)

The program has three subroutines that read information from the keyboard: the young adult subroutine, at line 100; the child subroutine, at line 200; and the adult subroutine, at line 300. In addition, the subroutine at line 1000 is reserved for processing the information. Each of the first three subroutines is designed to ask questions about one specific age category. During any given run of the program, only one or two of these three subroutines will be called. Let's see how this works.

Line 20 reads the age of the person who is responding to the program. The age is stored in the variable Y%:

    20 INPUT "HOW OLD ARE YOU? "; Y%

Lines 30, 40, and 50 all contain IF statements that test the value of
Y%. Line 30 tests to see if the age of the person falls within the
young adult range; if so, it calls the young adult subroutine:

    30 IF (Y% > = 17) AND (Y% < 20) THEN GOSUB 100

If the value of Y% is not within the young adult range, then line 30
results in no action at all. The program then moves on to line 40.

Lines 40 and 50 test to see if Y% is in the child range, or the adult
range, respectively:

    40 IF Y% < 17 THEN GOSUB 200
    50 IF Y% > = 21 THEN GOSUB 300

The important point is this: *only one* of these three lines (30, 40, or
50) will actually result in a transfer of control to a subroutine. The
decision of which subroutine to call depends on the value of Y%.
Whichever subroutine is called performs its information-
gathering task, and then returns control back to the line following
the GOSUB statement that made the call.

For example, let's say the person responding to this program is
31 years old. The input value 31 is stored in Y%. The IF conditions
at line 30 and 40 will not result in subroutine calls, so the program
will continue on to line 50. The condition:

    Y% > = 21

is true; 31 is greater than or equal to 21. So, line 50 sends control of
the program to the subroutine at line 300. The adult subroutine
asks two questions, stores the responses, and then returns control
back to the source:

    330 RETURN

As a result, the next line to be executed after line 330 will be line 60.

Let's look at the specific dialogue that would appear on the
screen. There are four questions, and four responses:

    HOW OLD ARE YOU? 31
    WHERE DO YOU WORK? XYZ CO
    WHAT IS YOUR JOB? PROGRAMMER
    WHAT IS YOUR NAME? PAT SMITH

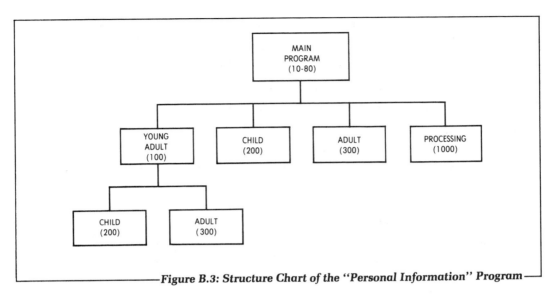

Figure B.3: Structure Chart of the "Personal Information" Program

The first of these four questions comes from the INPUT statement at line 20; the second and third questions are asked by the adult subroutine at line 300; and the final question is from line 60.

Now look at lines 70 and 80:

```
70 GOSUB 1000
80 END
```

Line 70 calls yet another subroutine (the one that processes the data), and line 80 ends the program. We can refer to the lines from 10 to 80 as the "main program" section of the program. These lines control the main action of the program by making subroutine calls. The subroutines, in turn, perform specific tasks, and then return control back to the main program section.

Figure B.3 shows a diagram of the organization of this program. This diagram is called a *structure chart,* and is a tool to help you visualize the action of the program. You can see that the four subroutines, represented by rectangles, are all under the control of the main program section. In addition, you can see that the young adult subroutine, at line 100, has two subroutines attached to it. This is because the young adult subroutine itself calls either the adult subroutine or the child subroutine to perform a job for it. This illustrates an important point: subroutines may call other subroutines in the same way that a main program may call a subroutine.

Let's examine the young adult subroutine. It begins, in line 110, by asking a question:

    110 INPUT "DO YOU W(ORK OR GO TO S(CHOOL <W OR S>? ";A$

This question will appear on the screen as:

    DO YOU W(ORK OR GO TO S(CHOOL <W OR S>?

The person must respond by typing either a W or an S. Line 110 stores the one-character response in the variable A$. Line 120 then tests the value of A$ in an IF statement. IF A$ does not contain either a "W" or an "S", then line 120 sends control of the program back up to line 110 to ask the question again:

    120 IF (A$ <> "S") AND (A$ <> "W") THEN GOTO 110

Then, depending on the value of A$, lines 130 and 140 call either the child subroutine or the adult subroutine. In other words, the young adult subroutine may result in one of two different dialogues. If the young adult goes to school, the dialogue will be taken partly from the child subroutine:

    DO YOU W(ORK OR GO TO S(CHOOL <W OR S>? S
    WHERE DO YOU GO TO SCHOOL? ABC SCHOOL

Or, if the young adult works, then the dialogue will come from the adult subroutine:

    DO YOU W(ORK OR GO TO S(CHOOL <W OR S>? W
    WHERE DO YOU WORK? XYZ CO
    WHAT IS YOUR JOB? PROGRAMMER

There are many advantages to organizing a program in this way. Here are three of the most important advantages:

1. By isolating certain specialized tasks in their own subroutines, you can make your program easier to understand, and, more importantly, easier to revise. Let's say, for example, that you decide you want to ask some additional questions about children. Since your program is organized in subroutines, you know exactly where to find the lines that deal with children—the child subroutine at line 200. The revision should take place exclusively within this subroutine and thus will affect neither the main program section nor the other subroutines of the program.

2. You can call a subroutine as many times as you need to; so by isolating common tasks in subroutines you avoid having to rewrite the same instructions over and over again.

3. While you are developing a program you can set aside lines for certain subroutines that you haven't written yet. For example, look at line 1000, the processing subroutine. This subroutine is just marked off with REM lines. In short, it does nothing when it is called—it simply returns control back to the main program. You may have any number of different plans for this subroutine. Perhaps you intend to produce a written record of the personal information. Or maybe you plan to store the information in a data file. Whatever your plans are, you haven't yet gotten around to implementing them. But the important point is this: you can run your program in its present state, test the subroutines that are already written, and make sure they do what you want them to do. Then, when you are ready, you can go back to the lines that you have reserved for the processing subroutine (starting at line 1000), and write the necessary instructions.

THE FOR/NEXT STATEMENT

One of the wonderful things about your computer is that it is willing to repeat the same task many hundreds or thousands of times without a word of complaint. We have seen ways of making the computer perform the same task repeatedly using the GOTO and GOSUB commands in BASIC.

For those instances when you know in advance exactly how many times you want a certain sequence of lines to be repeated, BASIC supplies the FOR/NEXT statements. We sometimes refer to the program structure created by these statements as a FOR loop, because they make your program loop back to perform the same instructions over and over. Let's look at an example.

The following FOR loop repeats a PRINT instruction 10 times:

```
10 FOR I = 1 TO 10
20    PRINT I
30 NEXT I
```

The result of these three lines will be the following column of ten numbers, displayed on your screen:

```
1
2
3
4
5
6
7
8
9
10
```

These FOR and NEXT instructions actually give several commands to the computer. We can think of these commands in four general steps:

1. Assign the value 1 to the variable I (sometimes called the *index* of the FOR loop).

2. Perform all the instructions between the FOR line and the NEXT line once. (In this case, there is only one line to perform—the PRINT instruction at line 20.)

3. Increase the value of I by 1.

4. If I is less than or equal to 10, then repeat the sequence of steps, starting from step #2, above. Otherwise, if I is greater than 10, then the action of the FOR loop is complete.

In this example, the value of the index, I, is increased by 1 each time the FOR loop repeats itself. BASIC lets us change the value of this incrementation by adding a STEP clause to the FOR instruction:

```
10 FOR I = 2 TO 10 STEP 2
20    PRINT I
30 NEXT I
```

The output result of these three lines is:

```
2
4
6
8
10
```

(If you don't see why, go back over the four steps described above. In step 1, I is initially assigned the value 2; in step 3, I is increased by 2 rather than 1.)

The BASIC FOR loop has another very important feature. The range of the index can be expressed as variables rather than explicit numbers. For example:

```
10 FOR I = V1 TO V2 STEP V3
       ...
50 NEXT I
```

In this case, the action of the FOR loop depends on the values stored in the variables V1, V2, and V3. The index, I, is initially assigned the value V1; then, for each repetition of the FOR loop, I is increased by the value of V3. The looping stops when I is greater than V2.

These variables give the FOR loop an open-ended quality; that is, the number of repetitions can be determined *during* the run of the program. The program might read values for V1, V2, and V3 from the keyboard or from a data file. Or, the program might calculate the values from other data.

A FOR loop is also an easy way to access the values of an array. Think back to the string array T1$, in which we stored the string values "ZERO" to "TEN". We could access those values as follows:

```
100 FOR I = 1 TO 10
110     PRINT T1$(I)
120 NEXT I
```

The output result would be:

```
ZERO
ONE
TWO
THREE
FOUR
FIVE
SIX
SEVEN
EIGHT
NINE
TEN
```

Notice that the variable I, which is incremented by the FOR loop, is used as the index into the array T1$. FOR loops and arrays can be an extremely powerful combination of programming elements.

The FOR loop in BASIC is clearly similar in function to the VisiCalc replication command; they both have the capacity of applying a formula repeatedly to a set of data items. However, the FOR command's open-ended quality makes it much more versatile and powerful than VisiCalc's /R command for many applications.

A FOR loop can contain any instructions at all between the FOR line and the NEXT line, including another FOR loop. FOR loops contained within other FOR loops are called *nested loops*:

```
10 FOR I = 1 TO 10
20    FOR J = 1 TO 10
        ...
50    NEXT J
60 NEXT I
```

The indentation illustrated above, while optional, will help you to see at a glance how the FOR loops are organized.

FUNCTIONS IN BASIC

Most versions of BASIC contain some of the same kinds of functions as the VisiCalc program; for example, the trigonometric functions, and the exponential functions are usually included. To duplicate some other VisiCalc functions, however, such as @SUM, @AVE, and @NPV, you have to write simple BASIC routines involving FOR loops and arrays. For example, if the array T1 contains 10 values, the following FOR loop will find the average of the values:

```
100 A = 0
110 FOR I = 1 TO 10
120    A = A + T1(I)
130 NEXT I
140 A = A/10
```

Line 120 accumulates the sum of the values in the array T1.

(Notice that A is *initialized* to 0 in line 100.) After the summation performed by the FOR loop, line 140 finds the average.

BASIC also has a number of valuable functions that operate on strings rather than on numbers. Your version of BASIC will have its own set of string functions.

Finally, most BASICs allow you to write one-line functions of your own. These are called user-defined functions. You create them with the DEF FN statement. The following two lines show examples of both the creation and subsequent use of such a function:

```
10 DEF FNS(X) = (X + 1)^2
20 PRINT FNS(5)
```

Line 10 defines the function FNS. This function receives a value in the "dummy" variable X, adds 1 to the value, and squares the result. Line 20 passes a value of 5 to the function, and prints the value returned from the function. The output result will be:

```
36
```

The program in Chapter 7 contains an interesting example of a user-defined function.

THE ASCII CODE

ASCII, *the American Standard Code for Information Exchange,* is used to translate the letters, digits, and special characters used by BASIC into the numeric code representation used to store them in the computer's memory. Each character corresponds to a number on the ASCII code. A partial ASCII table is shown in Figure B.4. The code actually contains values from 0 to 255, but the characters represented in the low and high ranges of the code tend to vary from one implementation to another.

BASIC has a function that translates an ASCII code number to an ASCII character. The function is CHR$. You can run the following short program to display the characters of the ASCII code:

```
10 FOR I = 0 TO 255
20    PRINT CHR$(I)
30 NEXT I
40 END
```

33	!	54	6	75	K
34	"	55	7	76	L
35	#	56	8	77	M
36	$	57	9	78	N
37	%	58	:	79	O
38	&	59	;	80	P
39	'	60	<	81	Q
40	(	61	=	82	R
41	)	62	>	83	S
42	*	63	?	84	T
43	+	64	@	85	U
44	,	65	A	86	V
45	-	66	B	87	W
46	.	67	C	88	X
47	/	68	D	89	Y
48	0	69	E	90	Z
49	1	70	F	91	[
50	2	71	G	92	\
51	3	72	H	93	]
52	4	73	I	94	^
53	5	74	J	95	_

Figure B.4: A Partial ASCII Code Table

APPENDIX C

SPECIAL KEYBOARD COMMANDS

INTRODUCTION

The specific keys or sequence of keys that you must press to move the VisiCalc cursor, and to erase or enter data from the edit line, vary from system to system. The names used in this book for these keyboard commands are as follows:

- The *direction* keys move the cursor—up, down, left, or right.
- The *escape* key erases one character (from the edit line) each time you press it.
- The *break* key erases the entire contents of the edit line, or cancels an entire command.
- The *return* key enters data from the edit line.

The following paragraphs explain how to execute these keyboard commands on the Apple® II; TRS-80™, models I and III; and the IBM® Personal Computer.

APPLE® II

The direction keys. The Apple II has only two direction keys, located at the right side of the keyboard, and labeled with left- and right-arrows, respectively. You can use these two keys to move the cursor in all four directions; pressing the space bar will toggle the keys back and forth into horizontal and vertical modes. A character displayed at the upper-right corner of the VisiCalc screen tells you which direction mode the keys are currently set at. A hyphen (-) indicates that the two keys will move the cursor to the right or to the left. An exclamation point (!) means that the keys will move the cursor up or down. Notice that this direction indicator changes each time you press the space bar.

The escape key. This key is labeled ESC, and is located at the upper-left corner of the keyboard.

The break key. The Apple II keyboard has no key labeled BREAK. To execute the break command, you must press two keys at once—the key labeled CTRL, and the C key. This sequence of keys is referred to as "control-C."

The return key. This key is labeled RETURN on the Apple II.

TRS-80™, MODELS I AND III

Direction keys. The TRS-80 computers have four separate direction keys, labeled with up-, down-, left-, and right-arrows, respectively.

The escape key. Use the key labeled CLEAR for this command.

The break key. Use the key labeled BREAK.

The return key. This key is labeled ENTER on the TRS-80 computers.

THE IBM® PERSONAL COMPUTER

The direction keys. The IBM Personal Computer has four distinct direction keys, located on the nine-key number pad.

The escape key. Use the back-space key for this command.

The break key. The key for this command is labeled SCROLL LOCK, and is located at the upper-right corner of the keyboard.

The enter key. Use the key labeled ◄⅃.

BIBLIOGRAPHY

Finkel, LeRoy, and Brown, Jerald R. *Data File Programming in BASIC: A Self-Teaching Guide.* New York: John Wiley & Sons, Inc., 1981.
 Teaches data file programming to beginners, in a "self-instruction" format. Includes chapters on both sequential files and random-access files.

Hergert, Douglas. *BASIC for Business.* Berkeley: Sybex, Inc., 1982.
 An introduction to BASIC programming. Includes many sample programs illustrating business applications.

Lien, David A. *The BASIC Handbook: Encyclopedia of the BASIC Computer Language.* 2nd ed. San Diego, Calif.: Compusoft Publishing, 1981.
 A reference work. Describes and illustrates all the elements of BASIC, and clarifies the confusing plethora of variations created by different commercial versions of BASIC.

Miller, Alan R. *BASIC Programs for Scientists and Engineers.* Berkeley: Sybex, Inc., 1981.
 A progression of advanced BASIC programs. Includes a chapter on BASIC sorting algorithms.

Tracton, Ken. *The Most Popular Subroutines in BASIC.* Blue Ridge Summit, Pa.: Tab Books, 1980.
 Includes listings and sample runs of dozens of essential BASIC algorithms.

Trost, Stan. *Doing Business with VisiCalc.* Berkeley: Sybex, Inc.,1982.
 Describes important business applications for the VisiCalc program, and supplies step-by-step commands for creating your own spreadsheets.

INDEX

The SYBEX Library

YOUR FIRST COMPUTER
by Rodnay Zaks   264 pp., 150 illustr., Ref. 0-045
The most popular introduction to small computers and their peripherals: what they do and how to buy one.

DON'T (or How to Care for Your Computer)
by Rodnay Zaks   222 pp., 100 illustr., Ref. 0-065
The correct way to handle and care for all elements of a computer system, including what to do when something doesn't work.

INTERNATIONAL MICROCOMPUTER DICTIONARY
140 pp., Ref. 0-067
All the definitions and acronyms of microcomputer jargon defined in a handy pocket-size edition. Includes translations of the most popular terms into ten languages.

FROM CHIPS TO SYSTEMS:
AN INTRODUCTION TO MICROPROCESSORS
by Rodnay Zaks   558 pp., 400 illustr. Ref. 0-063
A simple and comprehensive introduction to microprocessors from both a hardware and software standpoint: what they are, how they operate, how to assemble them into a complete system.

INTRODUCTION TO WORD PROCESSING
by Hal Glatzer   216 pp., 140 illustr., Ref. 0-076
Explains in plain language what a word processor can do, how it improves productivity, how to use a word processor and how to buy one wisely.

INTRODUCTION TO WORDSTAR™
by Arthur Naiman   208 pp., 30 illustr., Ref. 0-077
Makes it easy to learn how to use WordStar, a powerful word processing program for personal computers.

DOING BUSINESS WITH VISICALC®
by Stanley R. Trost   200 pp., Ref. 0-086
Presents accounting and management planning applications—from financial statements to master budgets; from pricing models to investment strategies.

EXECUTIVE PLANNING WITH BASIC
by X. T. Bui   192 pp., 19 illust., Ref. 0-083
An important collection of business management decision models in BASIC, including Inventory Management (EOQ), Critical Path Analysis and PERT, Financial Ratio Analysis, Portfolio Management, and much more.

BASIC FOR BUSINESS
by Douglas Hergert   250 pp., 15 illustr., Ref. 0-080
A logically organized, no-nonsense introduction to BASIC programming for business applications. Includes many fully-explained accounting programs, and shows you how to write them.

FIFTY BASIC EXERCISES
by J. P. Lamoitier   236 pp., 90 illustr., Ref. 0-056
Teaches BASIC by actual practice, using graduated exercises drawn from everyday applications. All programs written in Microsoft BASIC.

BASIC EXERCISES FOR THE APPLE
by J. P. Lamoitier   230 pp., 90 illustr., Ref. 0-084
This book is an Apple version of *Fifty BASIC Exercises*.

BASIC EXERCISES FOR THE IBM PERSONAL COMPUTER
by J. P. Lamoitier   232 pp., 90 illustr., Ref. 0-088
This book is an IBM version of *Fifty BASIC Exercises*.

INSIDE BASIC GAMES
by Richard Mateosian   352 pp., 120 illustr., Ref. 0-055
Teaches interactive BASIC programming through games. Games are written in Microsoft BASIC and can run on the TRS-80, Apple II and PET/CBM.

THE PASCAL HANDBOOK
by Jacques Tiberghien   492 pp., 270 illustr., Ref. 0-053
A dictionary of the Pascal language, defining every reserved word, operator, procedure and function found in all major versions of Pascal.

INTRODUCTION TO PASCAL (Including UCSD Pascal™)
by Rodnay Zaks   422 pp., 130 illustr. Ref. 0-066
A step-by-step introduction for anyone wanting to learn the Pascal language. Describes UCSD and Standard Pascals. No technical background is assumed.

APPLE® PASCAL GAMES
by Douglas Hergert and Joseph T. Kalash   376 pp., 40 illustr., Ref. 0-074
A collection of the most popular computer games in Pascal, challenging the reader not only to play but to investigate how games are implemented on the computer.

CELESTIAL BASIC: Astronomy on Your Computer
by Eric Burgess   320 pp., 65 illustr., Ref. 0-087
A collection of BASIC programs that rapidly complete the chores of typical astronomical computations. It's like having a planetarium in your own home! Displays apparent movement of stars, planets and meteor showers.

PASCAL PROGRAMS FOR SCIENTISTS AND ENGINEERS
by Alan R. Miller   378 pp., 120 illustr., Ref. 0-058
A comprehensive collection of frequently used algorithms for scientific and technical applications, programmed in Pascal. Includes such programs as curve-fitting, integrals and statistical techniques.

BASIC PROGRAMS FOR SCIENTISTS AND ENGINEERS
by Alan R. Miller   326 pp., 120 illustr., Ref. 0-073
This second book in the "Programs for Scientists and Engineers" series provides a library of problem-solving programs while developing proficiency in BASIC.

FORTRAN PROGRAMS FOR SCIENTISTS AND ENGINEERS
by Alan R. Miller   320 pp., 120 illustr., Ref. 0-082
Third in the "Programs for Scientists and Engineers" series. Specific scientific and engineering application programs written in FORTRAN.

PROGRAMMING THE 6809
by Rodnay Zaks and William Labiak   520 pp., 150 illustr., Ref. 0-078
This book explains how to program the 6809 in assembly language. No prior programming knowledge required.

PROGRAMMING THE 6502
by Rodnay Zaks   388 pp., 160 illustr., Ref. 0-046
Assembly language programming for the 6502, from basic concepts to advanced data structures.

6502 APPLICATIONS
by Rodnay Zaks   286 pp., 200 illustr., Ref. 0-015
Real-life application techniques: the input/output book for the 6502.

ADVANCED 6502 PROGRAMMING
by Rodnay Zaks   292 pp., 140 illustr., Ref. 0-089
Third in the 6502 series. Teaches more advanced programming techniques, using games as a framework for learning.

PROGRAMMING THE Z80
by Rodnay Zaks   626 pp., 200 illustr., Ref. 0-069
A complete course in programming the Z80 microprocessor and a thorough introduction to assembly language.

PROGRAMMING THE Z8000
by Richard Mateosian   300 pp., 124 illustr., Ref. 0-032
How to program the Z8000 16-bit microprocessor. Includes a description of the architecture and function of the Z8000 and its family of support chips.

THE CP/M® HANDBOOK (with MP/M™)
by Rodnay Zaks   324 pp., 100 illustr., Ref. 0-048
An indispensable reference and guide to CP/M—the most widely-used operating system for small computers.

MASTERING CP/M®
by Alan R. Miller   320 pp., Ref. 0-068
For advanced CP/M users or systems programmers who want maximum use of the CP/M operating system . . . takes up where our *CP/M Handbook* leaves off.

INTRODUCTION TO THE UCSD p-SYSTEM™
by Charles W. Grant and Jon Butah   250 pp., 10 illustr., Ref. 0-061
A simple, clear introduction to the UCSD Pascal Operating System; for beginners through experienced programmers.

A MICROPROGRAMMED APL IMPLEMENTATION
by Rodnay Zaks   350 pp., Ref. 0-005
An expert-level text presenting the complete conceptual analysis and design of an APL interpreter, and actual listing of the microcode.

THE APPLE CONNECTION
by James W. Coffron   228 pp., 120 illustr., Ref. 0-085
Teaches elementary interfacing and BASIC programming of the Apple for connection to external devices and household appliances.

MICROPROCESSOR INTERFACING TECHNIQUES
by Rodnay Zaks and Austin Lesea   458 pp., 400 illust., Ref. 0-029
Complete hardware and software interconnect techniques, including D to A conversion, peripherals, standard buses and troubleshooting.

SELF STUDY COURSES

Recorded live at seminars given by recognized professionals in the microprocessor field.

INTRODUCTORY SHORT COURSES:
Each includes two cassettes plus special coordinated workbook (2½ hours).

S10—INTRODUCTION TO PERSONAL AND BUSINESS COMPUTING
A comprehensive introduction to small computer systems for those planning to use or buy one, including peripherals and pitfalls.

S1—INTRODUCTION TO MICROPROCESSORS
How microprocessors work, including basic concepts, applications, advantages and disadvantages.

S2—PROGRAMMING MICROPROCESSORS
The companion to S1. How to program any standard microprocessor, and how it operates internally. Requires a basic understanding of microprocessors.

S3—DESIGNING A MICROPROCESSOR SYSTEM
Learn how to interconnect a complete system, wire by wire. Techniques discussed are applicable to all standard microprocessors.

INTRODUCTORY COMPREHENSIVE COURSES:
Each includes a 300-500 page seminar book and seven or eight C90 cassettes.

SB1—MICROPROCESSORS
This seminar teaches all aspects of microprocessors: from the operation of an MPU to the complete interconnect of a system. The basic hardware course (12 hours).

SB2—MICROPROCESSOR PROGRAMMING
The basic software course: step by step through all the important aspects of microcomputer programming (10 hours).

ADVANCED COURSES:
Each includes a 300-500 page workbook and three or four C90 cassettes.

SB3—SEVERE ENVIRONMENT/MILITARY MICROPROCESSOR SYSTEMS
Complete discussion of constraints, techniques and systems for severe environmental applications, including Hughes, Raytheon, Actron and other militarized systems (6 hours).

SB5—BIT-SLICE
Learn how to build a complete system with bit slices. Also examines innovative applications of bit slice techniques (6 hours).

SB6—INDUSTRIAL MICROPROCESSOR SYSTEMS
Seminar examines actual industrial hardware and software techniques, components, programs and cost (4½ hours).

SB7—MICROPROCESSOR INTERFACING
Explains how to assemble, interface and interconnect a system (6 hours).

SOFTWARE

BAS 65™ CROSS-ASSEMBLER IN BASIC
8″ diskette, Ref. BAS 65
A complete assembler for the 6502, written in standard Microsoft BASIC under CP/M®.

8080 SIMULATORS
Turns any 6502 into an 8080. Two versions are available for APPLE II.

APPLE II cassette, Ref. S6580-APL(T)
APPLE II diskette, Ref. S6580-APL(D)

FOR A COMPLETE CATALOG
OF OUR PUBLICATIONS

U.S.A.
2344 Sixth Street
Berkeley,
California 94710
Tel: (415) 848-8233
Telex: 336311

SYBEX-EUROPE
4 Place Félix-Eboué
75583 Paris Cedex 12
France
Tel: 1/347-30-20
Telex: 211801

SYBEX-VERLAG
Heyestr. 22
4000 Düsseldorf 12
West Germany
Tel: (0211) 287066
Telex: 08 588 163